THE
GRILLING
BOOK

To my father, Capt. A. E. Sinnes, the first person I ever saw having a great time preparing a meal, and to Tim Wolfe, the best natural griller I have ever met, for the many memorable meals we shared in greener days. May our children experience such gifts of food and friendship.

THE
GRILLING
BOOK

THE TECHNIQUES, TOOLS, AND TASTES
OF THE NEW AMERICAN GRILL

by

A. CORT SINNES *with Recipes by* **JAY HARLOW**
Illustrated by **EARL THOLLANDER**

Aris Books
Berkeley, Los Angeles

Copyright © 1985 by A. Cort Sinnes and Jay Harlow
Illustrations © 1985 by Earl Thollander

Library of Congress Cataloging in Publication Data:

Sinnes, A. Cort. 1952–
The grilling book.

Includes index.
1. Broiling. 2. Barbecue cookery. I Title.
TX687.S56 1985   641.7´6   84-24414
ISBN 0-943186-19-6

Aris Books are published by
Harris Publishing Company, Inc.
1621 Fifth Street
Berkeley, CA 94710
(415) 527-5171

Book trade distribution by Simon and Schuster, a division
of Simon & Schuster, Inc., Simon & Schuster Building,
Rockefeller Center, 1230 Avenue of the Americas, New York,
NY 10020.

Cover and book design by Sharon Smith Design
Composition in Trump by Linda Davis
of Ann Flanagan Typography
Printed by Maple-Vail Book Manufacturing Group

First printing March 1985

10 9 8 7 6 5 4 3
Manufactured in the United States of America

CONTENTS

RECIPE INDEX

SEASONAL GRILL MENUS

■ ■

Spring

Tomato, Cucumber, and Feta Cheese Salad

Grilled Leeks, *152*

Lamb Souvlaki Pita, *100*
with Tomatoes and Yogurt

Fresh Strawberry Ice Cream

Wine: young Cabernet Sauvignon or Merlot

Summer

Corn Grilled in Its Leaves, *153*

Grilled Ratatouille, *157*

Grilled Whole Salmon, *135*
or
Deviled Chicken, *114*

Assorted Melons

Wine: Italian Chardonnay, Macon-Villages,
or chilled Beaujolais

Fall

Grilled Scallop and Salmon Brochettes, *146*

Charcoal-grilled Duck, *118*
with Grilled Potato Wedges, *159*

Mixed Green Salad

Pears and Assorted Cheeses

Wine: California Chardonnay with the fish,
California Pinot Noir with the duck

Winter

Raw Oysters on the Half Shell

Grilled Artichoke Quarters, *154*

Grilled Dungeness Crab, *144*

Something Chocolate

Wine: Champagne or Chablis with the oysters;
Sauvignon Blanc with the crab

ACKNOWLEDGMENTS

To John Harris, publisher of Aris Books, and Managing Editor Mimi Luebbermann, for their dedication to the time-honored principles of publishing: a love of good books and an appreciation of the written word; to editor Carolyn Miller, for her skill and sense of humor; to Jay Harlow and Earl Thollander, for their complete involvement with the project and the professionalism they brought to it; to Katie and Brooke, my wife and daughter, for putting up with the inevitable bouts of crankiness that come with impending deadlines; and to: James McNair, for his help when it was most needed; Alan Steed, general manager of the Lazzari Fuel Company, for his information and genuine interest in the subject; Professor Conrad Bahre of the University of California at Davis, for sharing his far-ranging experience with mesquite; Loni Kuhn, for her willingness to share and illuminate; M.F.K. Fisher, for the use of her story "The Beachers," a prime example of her sensitivity and skill as a writer and world-class teacher; The Barbecue Industry Association; The Kingsford Company; Alice Waters for the graciousness she brought to yet another request from the curious; Chef Ed Porter and Wayne Hinkley, manager of Norman's restaurant in Berkeley, for their good food and for sharing their recipes in this book; Patricia Unterman, for her historical perspective on grilling; Kay Cochran, of Household Words, for keeping good books on food, now out of print, alive and well in her attic; and to Alan Freeland, Prince of the City, and the best friend a writer could have.

INTRODUCTION

Grilling foods over a charcoal fire is hardly a new phenomenon in this country, or in any other for that matter. What *is* new in America is an expanded approach to grilling that takes up where the backyard barbecue left off some years ago. More restaurants than ever have begun serving grilled foods—from simple fare to the most sophisticated—much to the delight of their patrons. This book takes a look at some of the new ways of using your own charcoal grill to produce a wide range of foods, many of which have their origins in cultures from Southeast Asia to the Mediterranean.

The Grilling Book takes a broad view of grilling—broader than what we as Americans have traditionally prepared over the glowing coals. The first chapter examines the history of grilling in this country, and shows that what is old is new again, particularly in the way of ethnic and regional grill specialties. Chapter 2 and Chapter 3 offer detailed information on the types of manufactured grills and the various fuels available, from briquets and mesquite to hardwood, and how to start a fire. Although this material may appear very basic, a surprising number of people refuse to approach a grill for the simple reason that they are not exactly sure of how to start a fire, or how to control it once it's going. Chapter 4, *A Griller's Guide to Good Eating*, which reflects the considerable knowledge of Jay Harlow, a professional grill cook, is a systematic treatment of the kinds of foods that can be successfully grilled—from meats, to vegetables, to bread and cheese. Many of these foods have become popular at grill restaurants; to our knowledge, this is the first time the methods for their preparation have been offered to the home griller in a substantial way. The emphasis is on basic techniques, with recipes that serve to illustrate them. Chapter 5, *Primeval Cuisine*, takes grilling from the backyard or balcony and into the wilds—to the forests and coasts—to discover the roots of this form of cooking. As such, grilling offers its practitioners a connection with the basic pleasures of life: a hot fire, good food, and the time to enjoy it.

This book is dedicated to a single principle: that one should experience a bit of pleasure on a daily basis. Quite simply, I know of no better way of achieving that pleasure than in the preparation and sharing of food—good food. Grilling, the most primitive of all cooking techniques, may also lay claim to being the most satisfying and, yes, the most pleasurable. To those schooled in the traditional techniques of *haute cuisine*, grilling may seem unsophisticated or rustic, but to me it is a lifelong method of having a little fun and being able to eat it afterwards. Grilling, in this regard, is akin to those two other great passions, gardening and fishing. For those of you who are tempted by this book to indulge in the pleasure of grilling, I wish you many enjoyable experiences.

CHAPTER ONE

▰▰▰▰▰▰▰▰▰▰▰▰▰▰▰▰▰▰▰▰

GRILLING: A TIMELESS TRADITION

Although the beginnings of the grill tradition are shrouded deep in the mists of mythology, we can be sure of one thing: Prometheus is to thank for the oldest cooking technique known to man. Prometheus, one of the great Zeus' sons, was also one of the Titans, known for their remarkable feats. Prometheus created mortal men and women from river clay at the same time his brother Epimetheus created the animal kingdom.

But the animals were snug and warm in their fur and feather coats, while Prometheus' mortals appeared a bit chilly running around in the altogether. Prometheus felt bad about this oversight and to remedy the situation stole some glowing embers from the sacred hearth of the gods, bringing them down from the heavenly kingdom to earth. His father, to put it mildly, was not pleased. The mortals, however, were thrilled. To show their thanks and respect for the great gift, the mortals regularly grilled a few members of the animal kingdom as sacrifices. The aroma wafted heavenward and pleased the gods, particularly Zeus, who had, of late, grown a little bored with a steady diet of ambrosia and nectar. The only thing the grill could offer was aroma, but because it had such a demanding clientele, this arrangement may have constituted the first grill "restaurant," and mortals have been grilling in one form or another ever since.

GRILLING, AMERICAN STYLE

■■■■■■■■■■■■■■■■■■■■■■■■■■■■■■■■■■

Although it is nearly impossible to accurately trace outdoor cooking to its prehistoric roots, it is fairly easy to chronicle the phenomenon in this country. The first Virginia settlers learned to cook over an open fire from the local Indians. British colonials took well to the culinary art and added a social dimension to it, holding gatherings that centered on outdoor cookery, something we still do today.

The Louisiana Acadians and the Texans, however, both claim title to introducing barbecuing into American cuisine. The Acadians say that the word *barbecue* comes from the French *barbe à queue*, or "from whiskers to tail," as in cooking the whole animal. They are the originators of Cajun cooking, which includes charcoal-smoked foods.

But the Texans remind us that the Spaniards were the first to learn this barbecue cookery from the Carib Indians. The Indians smoke-dried fish, fowl, and game on a green wood lattice over open fire or heated stones. The Spaniards named this lattice *barbacoa*, which is thought to have later become the word *barbecue*.

So the origin of the word *barbecue* is unclear. It's also hard to come up with a common definition that pleases all people. After all, you can go downtown to "eat some barbecue," you can put a steak "on the barbecue," you can also "barbecue a steak," or you can invite some friends over to "have a barbecue." When I presented the problem to my co-author Jay Harlow, a man who has spent considerable time in front of a professional charcoal grill, he came up with the following clarification of terms:

> *Grilling*, as it is used in this book, means cooking food directly over a charcoal or wood fire, with the food supported by a metal grill or a spit. What we call *grilling*, however, many people call *barbecuing*, and the backyard charcoal grill is almost universally referred to as a barbecue.
>
> The problem is, "barbecue" has various meanings in different parts of the country, and many of them have nothing to do with grilling. In the Southwest, a barbecue usually involves a whole animal cooked in a pit. In barbecue places from Kansas City to the Carolinas, smaller cuts of meats are slowly cooked in wood-fired ovens. An enormous culture has grown up around the phenomenon of barbecue, with countless local variations and loyal adherents to each. It would be pointless to say that cold-smoked beef brisket served up with bottled hot sauce *is* barbecue, and that pork ribs cooked over charcoal and smothered in a spicy red sauce *is not*, or vice versa.

Americans are getting very serious about their barbecue sauce.

> What most of the traditional barbecue techniques have in common is a long, slow cooking over a hardwood fire in a more or less enclosed space. About the closest home cooks can come to this (without building a brick oven or digging a pit in the backyard) is cooking in a covered grill by the indirect method (see page 46), or using a charcoal smoker (see page 29).

Strictly speaking, some barbecuing is a form of grilling, but much of the grilling technique in this book has nothing to do with traditional "barbecue." Grilling is a more general term: anything can be grilled, from all varieties of fish, game, poultry, and red meat, to vegetables and fruit, to cheese. Whether food (such as chicken or ribs) cooked on a charcoal grill and brushed with the "barbecue" sauces we offer on pages 74 and 75 constitutes true barbecue is a controversy we refuse to enter.

THE CROSS-CULTURAL GRILL

Many cultures can lay claim to their own unique style of grilling, but it seems to be those blessed with the warmest climates that have truly excelled in the endeavor. Anyone who has visited the Mediterranean, the Adriatic, parts of coastal Asia, Mexico, or the coasts of Central America knows the joys of regional grill cooking. That great grilling abounds in coastal areas with warm climates may be due to two simple facts: first, during warm weather, it's far more comfortable to cook and eat outdoors rather than heating up the interior of the house even more with a hot stove; and secondly, fish, plentiful in these regions, seems to lend itself particularly well to cooking over direct heat. In fact, many food professionals believe that fish and the charcoal grill were made for each other and that any other method of cooking fish is inferior.

It's not surprising then, that California, with its rich cultural mix, its proximity to Mexico, and its Mediterranean-type climate, thinks of itself as the home of the current mode of grilling in America (which is not to say that it is the home of that particular brand of grilling, the barbecue; no one in his right mind would take that away from the Southwest).

More than anything else, it is the presence of diverse cultures in California — each of which brought its own brand of grilling to the state—that has led to what is now being called "California cuisine." The fact that San Francisco was a thriving seaport for the approximately 100-year period starting in 1850 has had a profound effect on the eating habits of the state. The real inspiration for California cuisine came from the Japanese, Chinese, Indonesian, French, Italian, Greek, Mexican, Spanish, and Yugoslavian communities, the last-named particularly in San Francisco.

California cuisine is rooted in a diversity of traditional cuisines, all of which place importance on charcoal grilling. This, combined with a spirit of innovation and a dedication to fresh, high-quality ingredients, makes for some very interesting and enjoyable eating.

The genesis of the style of grilling discussed in this book—a style that is as common now in New York, Chicago, and Dallas as it is in San Francisco—can be divided into three waves: the Mediterranean and Mexican influence in early California, the immense rise in the popularity of outdoor cooking (à la suburban California) during the 1950s, and the current movement, started by young, creative California chefs during the 1970s.

THE FIRST WAVE

By 1850, a year after the famous influx of Gold Rush '49ers, a rough-and-tumble San Francisco boasted thirty-nine restaurants and sixty-six saloons. According to Doris Muscatine in her excellent book *Old San Francisco* (now unfortunately out of print), one part of the city looked like this:

> The waterfront area bustled with fish buyers, boardinghouse keepers, restaurateurs, and bargain-seeking poor folk, who threaded their way through garlands of drying mesh and islands of Sicilian fishermen sprawled in the sun, mending their nets with crude wooden shuttles. The customers dealt directly with the boatmen for their purchases or bought from wharfside

stalls. The returning fishermen customarily breakfasted on deck, filling the dockside with the aroma of fresh fish grilling over charcoal. (New York: G. P. Putnam's Sons, 1975)

The three oldest surviving grill restaurants in San Francisco are Tadich Grill (opened in 1849 as the Wigwam and one of California's one hundred oldest businesses); Jack's, opened in 1864 and still serving some of the best food in America from its original Sacramento Street location (interrupted only briefly when the 1906 earthquake and fire forced it to move across town); and Sam's Grill, which opened in 1867. In the course of a century or so, these old-guard grills have established a grill style of their own, one that is simplicity itself: fresh local fish (brushed with a little oil and dusted with paprika) and shellfish, chops, and steaks grilled over charcoal, usually *sans* sauce. Although each has a unique personality and subtle stylistic differences, they have in common a very honest approach to serving local specialties. It is important to note that the freshest quality ingredients combined with an honest and simple method of preparation have kept these restaurants crowded for over one hundred years. As currently popular—and even "trendy"—as grilling may be today, it is simply not a new phenomenon. The newer grill restaurants have brought their own styles to the existing San Francisco grill tradition. The individual influences may be from the Southwest (Tex-Mex), or the Cajun, Japanese, Italian, or French cuisines, but the core of the eating experience—fresh, quality ingredients cooked over a charcoal fire—remains the same.

Other historical observations help to put the current grill phenomenon in perspective. Again, from Doris Muscatine's *Old San Francisco:*

Excellent eating places were crammed into the bazaarlike atmosphere of the market area much in the manner of the Paris bistros in the original Les Halles. In 1854 a Parisian-style rotisserie on Kearny Street roasted to order poultry, meats, fish, and game bought on the premises or in the nearby stalls. Attached to the prongs of a three-rod iron grill, the succulent roasts turned slowly over a bed of coals filling a six-foot-wide fireplace. The charge for cooking a duck or chicken came to 50 cents, and all items had to be taken elsewhere for eating.

Yugoslavians, particularly Dalmatians (Dalmatia has long since been incorporated into Yugoslavia but was once a distinct region on the Adriatic Coast) figured prominently in many of the earliest San Francisco grill restaurants: John Tadich, who bought the Wigwam restaurant in 1882 and changed the name to Tadich, was a Dalmatian immigrant.

Although it would be hard to find a Dalmatian grill chef in San Francisco today, the straightforward principles and simple grilling practices of the original chefs have been faithfully handed down from one generation of grillers to the next. It is interesting to note how the current practitioners of grilling have patterned their techniques after the original sources of inspiration. Patricia Unterman, restaurant critic for the *San Francisco Chronicle* and partner in the very popular Hayes Street Grill, says it wasn't until she visited Yugoslavia that she had a real appreciation for simple grilling techniques, especially with regard to fish. Upon returning home she decided that San Franciscans were ready for the next wave of Dalmatian-inspired cooking, and she was right. For Unterman, the most important practice she observed and brought home was that of not overcooking the fish, a complaint she has of some of the older grill establishments. She admits having to "educate" her customers as to the definition of overdone, done, and underdone fish. When her restaurant first opened, many entrées were sent back to the grill with the request for "just a few more minutes on each side, please," but that has subsided as people have come to enjoy the true, fresh flavor of the fish itself, combined with a hint of mesquite charcoal aroma.

THE SECOND WAVE

■▰■▰■▰■▰■▰■▰■▰■▰■▰■▰■▰■▰■▰■▰■▰■

The post-World-War II housing boom in California had a good deal to do with the popularity of grilling today. A look through *Sunset* (*the* voice of western living) and other "home and garden" magazines from the war years reveals some interesting material.

In the 50's, built-in barbecues were a common feature in many backyards.

Just prior to the war, houses were being constructed, for the most part, in fairly classic interpretations of traditional styles (Colonial, Tudor, Norman, Mediterranean, and what-have-you). During the war, a number of young architects decided it was time to "break the box" and open the Western home to the outdoors. In issue after issue of *Sunset* and similar periodicals from the early 1940s through the fifties, westerners were treated to a new vision of what life could be like in sunny California after the war.

What replaced the traditional "box" house was an open "living space." Concrete slab floors (with radiant heat) went right through "window walls" to become outdoor patios. Sliding glass doors brought the outdoors in, and vice versa. The patio became as much a part of the house as any other room; it is not by coincidence that landscape architects of the era began calling gardens "outdoor rooms." There were utility areas (clotheslines, dog pens, and places for the garbage cans), play areas (with flower beds that were raised so as not to be damaged by careening tricyclists), and last but not least, outdoor cooking and eating areas, with built-in "barbecues," sinks, and tables and chairs.

Over the course of years, this new trend in living became the vision of the "good life"—especially appealing to a generation eager to put the war era behind them. There's hardly a native-California baby-boomer around who doesn't remember regularly eating family dinners outdoors during the warm months of the year. In our collective memories are visions of the old man with a platter of hamburgers or T-bone steaks in one hand and a "sundowner" in the other. In many ways, it *was* the good life, come home to roost in our backyards.

THE THIRD WAVE

If we accept the fact that grilling foods over a hot charcoal fire wasn't invented yesterday, it's safe to proceed to Berkeley, California, circa 1971. Anyone who follows trends in food and

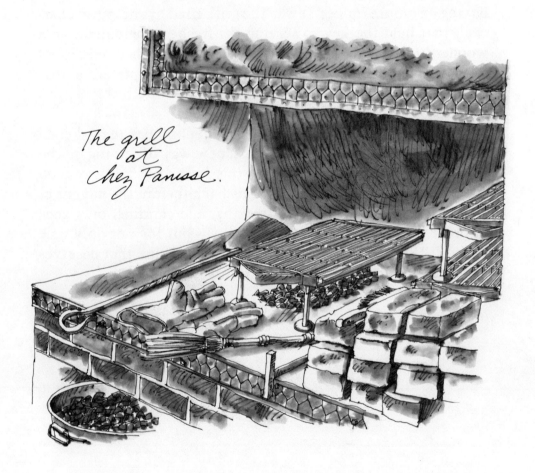

The grill at Chez Panisse.

restaurants may already know the Chez Panisse story by heart; its history has been well chronicled from coast to coast. Nonetheless, genius always deserves to be recognized, and Alice Waters' Chez Panisse, and what hence has been termed "California cuisine," has a great deal to do with today's increased interest in grill cooking and the use of fresh local ingredients in new and interesting ways.

Alice Waters is one of the founders of "California cuisine": nearly all the proprietors of the most popular "bar and grill" restaurants in the San Francisco Bay Area today at one time or another passed through the portals (either as chefs, apprentices, or at the very least, as customers) of Waters' restaurant. Her menus were built around locally grown and produced foods (fish, goat cheeses, a staggering array of produce, kid, California caviar and oysters—you name it) in a simple style that revealed the true nature of the food itself. No fancy sautéing or baking *en croute* for her. It was the grill, fired by mesquite charcoal, that held the key to serving the freshest ingredients in a wonderful way. It was an idea whose time had come, as witnessed by the scores of imitators and interpreters across America who quickly followed in the wake of Chez Panisse's success.

The "new American grilling phenomenon" has reawakened our tastebuds and introduced us to a new way of serving up the best of our local foodstuffs. That this is exactly the way food was enjoyed a couple of generations back (before the advent of the refrigerated rail car, flash freezing, and canning) only goes to prove that "what's old is new again"—but it's not only new again, it is also a delicious and healthful cuisine that deserves to be experienced by anyone who truly enjoys eating.

CHAPTER TWO

WHERE TO PUT THE FIRE

In the beginning, when Prometheus brought the gift of fire to his mortals, the immediate solution was to contain it within a ring of stones. Today, however, as is often the case in the marketplace, there is an extensive and sometimes confusing array of grills from which to choose. The entire spectrum of these products, however, can be divided into two categories: covered and uncovered. Aside from that important distinction, the choices vary significantly only in size.

There are strong feelings regarding covered and uncovered grills. People who don't like covered grills frequently complain of the fact that you can't move the grill (or the bed of coals) up or down to control the temperature in most models. And many re-sent the fact that to be used properly, the way they were designed to be used, covered kettle grills should be be used with the cover on. People who endorse covered grills say that once you get used to cooking on them, and to their versatility in terms of smoking and cooking large roasts and whole turkeys and chickens, it is hard to go back to the limitations of the open grill.

I feel that an open grill is best for fish, steaks, or paillards—in short, anything that doesn't demand much time on the grill. With the addition of a rotisserie, you can easily cook roasts and whole turkeys or chickens. Covered grills, on the other hand, are excellent for foods that require longer cooking times, and are of real service with fatty foods such as chicken or ribs. Of course, one could solve the problem by having one of each type of grill, but that may be a little excessive for most people. Given a choice, I would opt for a combination drop-in or portable model, like the ones illustrated on pages 29, 31, and 32, where you have the best of both worlds: an optional cover *and* an adjustable firebox. It's important to note that the grill surface of the drop-in models is much larger than that of most other grills, making it easy to cook a whole fish, for example, or cook for a crowd.

UNCOVERED GRILLS
■▰■▰■▰■▰■▰■▰■▰■▰■▰■▰■▰■▰■▰■▰■▰■▰■▰■

Hibachis

The small, amost unbelievably low-priced hibachi has obvious drawbacks when it comes to size, but for one or two people, or for preparing hors d'oeuvres right on the table, it can't be beat (see page 23). Hibachis can be set up almost anywhere outdoors, including fire escapes, back stairs, and fourth-floor balconies— you can even use one inside your fireplace. Ex-Boy Scouts and other "be prepared" types have been known to keep one, along with other grilling equipment, wrapped in a gunnysack in the trunk of the car for use on picnics.

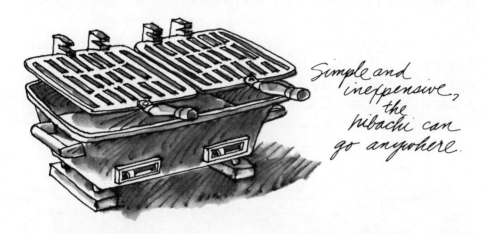

Simple and inexpensive, the hibachi can go anywhere.

Portable Braziers

You don't see as many of these around as you used to. This was the classic "barbecue" of the 1950s. Its grill may get a little unsteady with age, but it is adjustable, and the half-round hood allows for the attachment of a motorized rotisserie. The grill is large enough to handle fairly large amounts of food. It's somewhat difficult to clean the ashes out of the firebox.

The portable brazier was the standard grill a few years back, often outfitted with a hood and rotisserie.

Grills for Rent

If you're planning a party for ten or more people, featuring food hot from the grill, it's probably a good idea to check with your local rental service to see whether they stock these large portable grills. In the long run, renting one will make the food preparation a lot easier. Guests won't have to eat in shifts, and the presence of a large grill, in itself, creates a festive impression. Rental services almost always provide delivery and pickup service, usually a good idea with such a bulky piece of equipment.

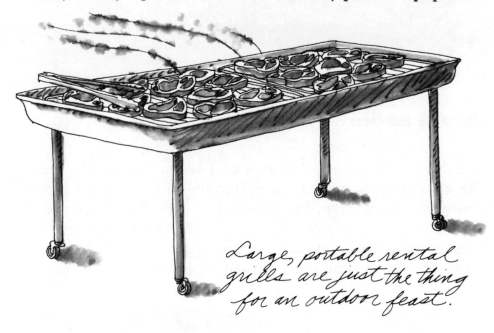

Large, portable rental grills are just the thing for an outdoor feast.

Indoor Built-in Grills

To have an honest-to-goodness indoor charcoal grill, right there in your kitchen, would have to be some kind of fun. Even to contemplate it indicates that you are a seriously committed griller, wanting the opportunity to grill year round. Obviously, there's a great deal to consider from the construction standpoint: it's about the same as adding a fireplace to a room. But if you're doing a major kitchen remodeling or building a new home, it's something to think about. I, for one, harbor fantasies of a kitchen fireplace-and-grill combination. The drop-in unit described on page 28 is one way to achieve an indoor grill; restaurant suppliers offer professional models that can be used in homes at, naturally, professional prices.

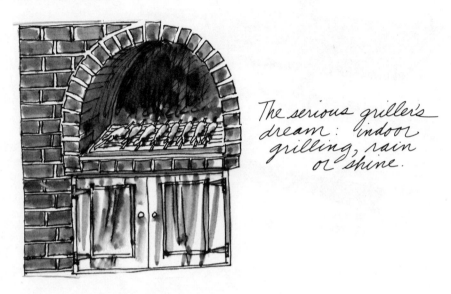

The serious griller's dream: indoor grilling, rain or shine.

Indoor Fireplace Grills

If a built-in indoor grill is out of the question, consider a fireplace grill. The only thing about grilling in your fireplace is that you're liable to get more or less permanent grease stains on the masonry, make the living room smell like the kitchen, and probably dribble some sauce on the carpet. But what are these concerns when you just have to grill a fresh fish in the middle of a snowstorm?

These new grills are patterned after European models. Alice Waters of Chez Panisse tells us that she and a friend in Italy are importing a Tuscan fireplace grill that has a built-in pan to collect drippings (see page 26). For ordering information, write to Singer & Foy Wines, 1821 Powell Street, San Francisco, CA 94133.

Alice Waters' Tuscan fireplace grill.

COVERED GRILLS

■■■■■■■■■■■■■■■■■■■■■■■■■■■■■■■■■■■■■■■

The addition of a cover significantly changes the process of grilling. For one thing, when the cover is in place, flare-ups rarely occur, due to the reduced oxygen level. This, in many people's mind, is a big plus, resulting in far fewer burned meals. The second important difference is that hot air circulates around the food, cooking it as if it were in an oven at the same time it is being grilled. Because of this, total cooking time is reduced in a covered grill, as opposed to an open grill. And covered grills do give food more of a smoky flavor than do open grills.

Kettle-type Grills

These are far and away the most popular of the covered grills and, according to most people, with good reason. These grills come in four basic sizes, with the smallest intended for occasional picnic and camp cooking. The kettle-type grill was designed to be used with the cover on; in fact, the manufacturers discourage the use of the grill without it. Neither the grill nor the firebox is adjustable, so you are stuck with coals a set distance (approximately 5 inches) away from the grill, a fact that annoys some people. Be that as it may, this is the grill of choice for most outdoor cooks, who extol its virtues of versatility and ease of use (see page 46).

Probably the most popular grill in America — and for good reason.

Kamados

These imports from Japan are constructed of very heavy clay and are an interesting variation on the covered-grill theme. As in a kettle-type grill, there is both a top and bottom vent for adjustable temperature control, and the Kamados come in four different sizes. However, the grill in this case is even farther away from the fire than in the kettle-type models. The porosity of the clay makes for moister heat, which is great for smoking and baking, but not so good for achieving the crispy exterior on foods that many grill enthusiasts crave. The devil to clean out, Kamados are often advertised as "lasting indefinitely," which may be stretching it a bit. Eventually, especially if left out in the elements, some part of the Kamado will begin to disintegrate or break—usually not until after many years of service, however. A word of warning: watch the cover when it's open, especially around kids. It's very heavy, and when it comes down unexpectedly, you will know it.

Made of clay, the Kamado is an interesting covered grill variation -- not without its limitations -- but great for all types of smoking.

Drop-in Grills

Permanent outdoor grills are not nearly as popular now as they were a generation ago, but with the rekindled interest in grilling, who knows? Large lumber, hardware, or do-it-yourself stores usually stock a catalog containing drop-in grills, which have to be special-ordered. The disadvantage, of course, is that you have to have something to drop them into, like a permanent outdoor brick counter. The units are surprisingly inexpensive. They feature an adjustable firebox, and both the grill and firebox are manufactured to stand up to heavy-duty use. Add-on accessories include rotisseries and hoods, which makes them very versatile. The extra-large grill area makes it convenient to cook for crowds.

Easy to customize, the ready-made, drop-in grill is both affordable and readily available.

Charcoal Smokers

Smoking units for the home chef are becoming more available. One model, known as the Cajun Cooker, has been popular for years in the South. Another unit called the Smoke 'n Pit is making its appearance across the country. Even though the Smoke 'n Pit is a multiuse "outdoor kitchen" (it can be used as a covered grill, for roasting, smoking, or steaming), these smokers are really a variation of grilling and should be treated as such, rather than as a replacement for grilling.

In their favor, these smokers probably offer the closest reproduction of the famous barbecue places of the Southwest and Midwest states: a way to cook meats over a low, smoky fire for long periods of time. You can turn out some fabulous food using these cookers—especially large cuts of beef, venison and other wild game, pork, and the like—but don't expect them to perform at their best as a standard charcoal grill. If you go in for smoking foods in a big way, the ideal would be to have a standard charcoal grill *and* and charcoal smoker.

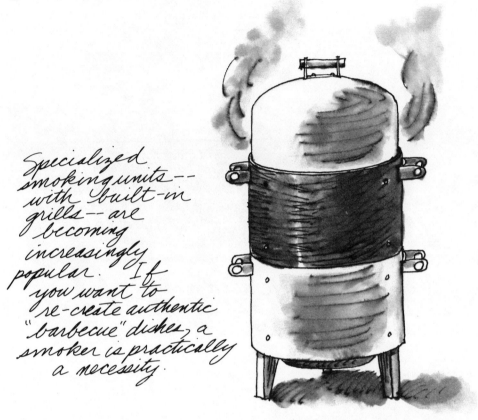

Specialized smoking units— with built-in grills—are becoming increasingly popular. If you want to re-create authentic "barbecue" dishes, a smoker is practically a necessity.

Electric and Gas-fired Grills

Up until this point I have tried to maintain a modicum of impartiality, but when it comes to electric and gas-fired grills, with their lava-rock "coals," I've got to be honest with you: they just go against the grain of how I perceive the pleasures of grilling. This is not to say that you can't turn out some great-tasting food on these units; I've been told you can. But it seems to me a little like sitting in front of one of those fake ceramic-log fireplace units with the gas jets roaring away on a cold winter's night; somehow it's just not the same as a real fire. Yes, they are easy to start and there are no ashes to clean up (you should clean them occasionally, however, the same as you would your kitchen oven), and you can add smoking chips (see page 50) if you want a little additional flavor, but, really, they *are* a horse of a different color.

Rectangular Grills

Other manufacturers have tried to beat the kettle-type grill at its own game, offering a less spherically shaped unit with the addition of an adjustable grill. It's a good combination unit, but surprisingly hard to find. Kettle aficionados say the rectangular shape doesn't disperse the heat as evenly as the kettle-shaped grill, and it definitely is more difficult to clean the ashes out of the rectangular grill currently on the market.

The addition of an adjustable grill makes this covered grill even more versatile.

Wagon-type Grills

Wagon-type units are the most expensive of the portable charcoal grills. In many ways, the added expense is warranted, especially if you grill frequently. To borrow from an old saying, some grills are built for comfort, and some are built for speed, and the wagon types are definitely built for comfort. Usually constructed of heavy-duty materials (some even have cast-iron grills, the preferred choice of professional grillers), they offer a great deal of versatility—an adjustable firebox, rotisseries, an optional hood—and often "standard options" such as temperature gauges and lighted grills.

Wagon-type grills are often made of heavy-duty materials—for the avid—and often griller.

TOOLS OF THE TRADE

A familiar accessory for home grilling is a set of long-handled tools, usually a spatula and fork, and sometimes a basting brush, and perhaps even salt and pepper shakers on long handles. These sets can be quite impressive looking, with turned wooden handles, leather thongs for hanging, and so on. Unfortunately, they are not always good tools. The spatulas invariably have small blades, and the forks often have thick, dull tines.

There are better tools available, however, and in some cases they are even less expensive. The best source of professional-quality hand tools is a restaurant supply house (look in the yellow pages). Cookware shops and catalogs are also beginning to carry professional tools. Following are the essential tools for grill cooking:

Spring-loaded tongs Professional grill cooks do a lot of their work with spring-loaded stainless-steel tongs. With a little practice, you will find you can turn almost any cut of meat, as well as brochettes of seafood, whole fish, small game birds—in fact, just about anything but fish fillets—with these tongs. Because they are spring-loaded, they are much easier to handle than the scissor-action tongs found in most home kitchens.

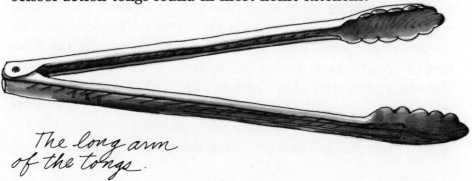

The long arm of the tongs.

Offset spatula Next to tongs, the other indispensable tool of professional grill cooks is a long-bladed offset spatula. These come in a range of sizes, but the most useful size has a blade 7½ by 3 inches, large enough to lift a whole delicate fish fillet. Spatulas made for home use are rarely more than 4 or 5 inches long,

The pro's choice: an offset spatula.

big enough for a hamburger, but not for a whole rockfish fillet. The home models also tend to be rather flimsy. With a proper professional spatula, you can use the length and stiffness of the blade to simultaneously scrape and lift the fillets off the grill.

Skewers A good skewer must not only hold small pieces of food together, it must also keep them from rotating on the skewer when the skewer is turned—otherwise every time you go to turn the skewer of food, the food will move around so that it's always being cooked on the same side. For this reason, look for skewers that are not round when viewed straight on.

Metal skewers are durable and useful for cooking large brochettes, especially of red meats. Small wooden or bamboo skewers have the advantage of not getting as hot as the metal variety; they also leave a smaller hole. However, the exposed ends of wooden skewers will burn if left on the fire long enough. To delay this, soak them in water before skewering the food. And if you're now saying to yourself, "But aren't bamboo skewers round, and didn't he just say. . ." Yes, they are round, but their smaller size makes it possible to use two skewers for each brochette of meat or vegetables, parallel to each other and spaced ¼ to ½ inch apart, to keep the food stationary.

The multi-purpose skewer.

Besides their primary use, a small skewer is an excellent tool for probing the flesh of cooking meat (especially fish and chicken) to check on its degree of doneness. With a little bit of practice, you can use the point of a skewer to tell when the center of the thickest part of a piece of fish is barely done, then whisk it off the grill before it overcooks (see page 128).

Basting brush A good-sized brush is useful for oiling the grill before heating, for brushing a little oil on fish before cooking, and for applying marinades or sauces to food already on the grill. A 2- or 3-inch paint-brush type with natural bristles is the most useful size. Long-handled brushes are available if you prefer to work a greater distance from the fire.

■ A few other common grill tools are not essential, but they are popular:

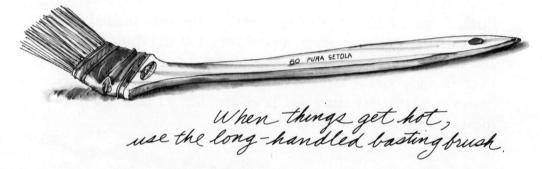

When things get hot, use the long-handled basting brush.

Hinged fish grill One piece of equipment often mentioned in cookbooks as essential to grilling fish is a folding grill. This is typically a pair of thin wire grills with long handles, joined by a hinge on the side opposite to the handle. The idea is to place one or more pieces of fish (whole, fillets, steaks, or what have you) between the two grills and clamp the handles together. The whole arrangement can then be turned easily or moved around to hotter or cooler parts of the grill.

A hinged grill is useful for cooking a whole butterflied fish or some other large piece that will be cut up into serving pieces later. It is not really necessary if you keep your grill clean and well oiled and keep the fish pieces to a manageable size. The hinged grill *is* very helpful if you are cooking slices of vegetables, or other small pieces of food not on skewers.

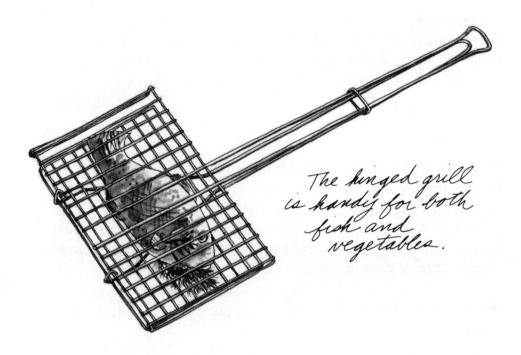

The hinged grill is handy for both fish and vegetables.

Fork Some cooks prefer to use a fork rather than hinged tongs for handling steaks or other cuts of meats. If the tines are good and sharp, they can serve the same function as a testing skewer, to probe the cooking meat to check on doneness. Keep in mind, however, that every time you poke another set of holes in the meat, more juices will run out.

Every good grill needs one ... a long handled fork.

Wire brush A long-handled wire brush will make short work of cleaning a grill, especially if you brush it while it is still hot. Any debris will fall into the fire and disintegrate. After you use it a few times, the brush is not that attractive to look at, but it certainly is easier to use one than to try and clean a greasy grill when it's cold. It's a good idea to get into the habit of brushing the grill clean immediately after you take the food off.

The wire grill brush ... for brushing after every meal.

Thermometers There are several ways to tell when specific foods are done (see page 62), but none is quite as precise and objective as a thermometer. The instant-read thermometer is probably the easiest to use. It is similar to a standard meat thermometer, but it registers the internal temperature of a food immediately. For accuracy, however, the food must be at least an inch thick. Standard meat thermometers are just as useful as instant-read thermometers, but they must be left in the food for several minutes in order to register the correct temperature. Pit thermometers are of little use in grilling, with the exception of cold smoking, where the temperature of the smoke must be maintained at a constant level; in this case, pit thermometers are invaluable. Some covered grills include thermometers in the hood, which is convenient for cold smoking.

For large roasts, a meat thermometer is indispensable.

CHAPTER THREE

■■■■■■■■■■■■■■■■■■■■■■■■■■■■■■■■

THE GIFT OF FIRE

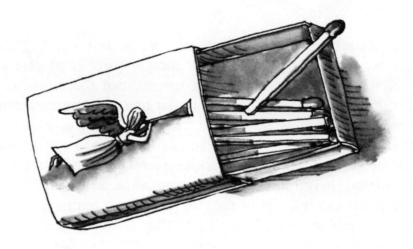

Doubtless the first grilled feasts were roasted over a fire made of wood rather than charcoal. The superior burning properties of charcoal were discovered a little later. According to the Kingsford Company, "charcoal was probably 'discovered' shortly after fire itself, when a burning log inadvertently was covered with sand or other debris. It continued smoldering for a while, and then went out. But the magic had been done. It had turned into charcoal. Whoever dug the log up and relit it discovered that the fire burned hotter, with less smoke, and cooked food better." Charcoal has been manufactured around the world for centuries, in what we now call "lump" form, particularly by coastal cultures and partly as a solution to a scarcity of wood to use for fuel.

Charcoal starts out as wood, but as a result of the process of "burning" without oxygen, it becomes an entirely different substance with its own burning characteristics. Wood burned in the presence of oxygen will simply burn itself into ash. Take away almost all the oxygen while the wood is "burning" (smoldering is more like it), and the wood (technically cellulose) is burned away, leaving carbon, or charcoal; and carbon, or charcoal, burns differently than wood: hotter, longer, and with very little flame or smoke.

The charcoal briquet industry is a relatively new phenomenon. It had its beginnings in 1923, when Henry Ford decided to manufacture his own wood alcohol, which was necessary to automobile production. A by-product of the alcohol was lump charcoal. At that time, the use of charcoal both as a cooking and as a heating element was beginning to be replaced by gas ranges and heaters. It was decided to manufacture charcoal in the form of briquets, which were sold as an industrial fuel, and as a grilling medium for the food industry (no less a personage than Thomas Alva Edison designed the first charcoal-briquet plant for his friend, Henry Ford).

The market for Ford's briquets never equalled the supply, however, and the plant was sold in 1951. A release by the Kingsford Company explains what was to become the next phase of America's culinary history:

> In 1953 and 1954, the Kingsford Company launched a major sales promotion. A 4-in-1 barbeque kit was offered to the general public. The kit consisted of a grill, a 5-pound bag of charcoal briquets, a can of lighter fluid and a heavy-duty cardboard carrying case.
> The outdoor grill, like the canasta party, and a phenomenon called rock and roll, took the country by storm. . . .

And as the sun sets on our canasta party, we now leave the history lesson and move on to the present concern: which type of charcoal to use for tonight's dinner.

CHARCOAL BRIQUETS VS. LUMP CHARCOAL

Presently there are two types of fuel commercially available for outdoor cooking: charcoal briquets and natural lump charcoal. And in that seemingly simple statement there rages a controversy. But before considering the controversy, let alone deciding which side you're on, it's necessary to know a little more about the two choices.

Lump charcoal is just that: lumps of charcoal, produced by smoldering wood (see page 43). The lumps of charcoal may have originally been oak, mesquite, maple, cherry, or some other hardwood. But the essential characteristic of lump charcoal is its simple carbon composition; it has no additives of any kind and has not been processed into any shape other than the way it naturally breaks into lumps.

Charcoal briquets are made up of charcoal, starch, coal, and perhaps a few other chemical ingredients to enhance their lighting and burning capabilities. Sodium nitrite, for example, is added by many manufacturers, because as it heats up it gives off oxygen and makes the briquets light faster.

The manufacturing process goes like this: sawdust and otherwise unusable scraps from a lumber mill are put into a carbonization furnace, where the volatile elements are burned off, leaving only the carbon behind. The carbon is then mixed with a starch binder, ground coal (either anthracite or lignite), and other ingredients a particular manufacturer might deem necessary. The mixture is quite moist at this point (approximately 32 percent moisture) and is formed into briquets as the mixture is forced between two opposing wheels (each wheel having a depression equal to one-half the familiar briquet shape). The briquets then travel by conveyer belt to a dryer, where their moisture content is reduced and, from there, are tumbled into bags to be shipped off.

Although the carbon component of most briquets is derived from lumber-mill by-products, carbon can be made from any organic substance—corn cobs, walnut shells, bones—you name it. There is only a handful of manufacturers of charcoal briquets in this country that use hardwood by-products exclusively for the carbon component of their briquets. One of them is the Humphrey Charcoal Corporation in Brookville, Pennsylvania.

Mr. R. C. Humphrey is a man who knows his charcoal; his family-run business has been making the product since 1944. He can explain, for example, one of the major marketing advantages of briquets: "The stores that sell charcoal would rather have the briquets because they take up less shelf or floor space. You can get twice as many 20-pound bags of charcoal briquets into the same space as you can 20-pound bags of lump charcoal. Because the briquets tend to settle down and nest together, they make a much more compact bag. Floor space equals profits in the super-market business. Not only that, but whereas you can load 22 tons of briquets into one truckload, you can only load 12 or 14 tons into the same-sized truck, so shipping costs are much higher for lump charcoal."

Lump charcoal is expensive and harder to find than briquets, but that doesn't deter its devotees, who say that once you get used to lump charcoal, you won't go back to briquets. Lump charcoal enthusiasts say that the fire produced by it is hotter, and therefore better at searing in the juices of fish, poultry, or red meat; the fire also stays hot longer, and the smoke adds a pleasant aroma to the finished product. Their major complaint about briquets is their "off" odor, which is due to the coal or other ingredients used in their manufacture. One slight disadvantage of lump charcoal is the lack of uniformity in the size of the lumps; you may need to break up large lumps with a hatchet so that the fire will burn evenly.

Lump versus ...

charcoal briquet ... a burning controversy.

MESQUITE CHARCOAL

Although several different types of lump charcoal are sold in this country, mesquite is by far the most available. This is due, in part, to the fact that members of the mesquite family (botanically the genus *Prosopis*) are what in horticultural circles is referred to as "weed trees," meaning that their numbers multiply and thrive with very little or no attention from the human species. Other forms of lump charcoal, made from apple, oak, hickory, or other woods, are available in very limited supplies in regional areas. If you can find some, by all means give it a try, if for no other reason than to experiment.

Mesquite trees and shrubs are native to both North and South America, primarily in arid regions. Because they hybridize readily among themselves, there is considerable variation within the family, making the classification into species difficult, if not impossible. The fact that mesquite is thought of as a weed tree has not kept it from being useful. According to *Plants for Dry Climates*, mesquite has "long supplied desert dwellers with shade and shelter, fuel for fires, building materials, food for livestock, and shredded bark for making baskets. Their beans are ground into food (the *pinole* of Mexico). Bees make an excellent honey from their flowers" (Mary Duffield and Warren Jones [Tucson, AZ: HP Books, 1981]).

The mesquite is first stacked into large pyramids...

The Lazzari Fuel Company of Brisbane, California, is one of this country's largest importers of Mexican mesquite charcoal—they've been importing it since 1944. Most of the charcoal is made by the Yaqui Indians on their reservation near Vicom in the Mexican state of Sonora, where the tradition of mesquite charcoal-making is passed on from one generation to another. The industry is heavily controlled by the Mexican government, which sets the prices and grants exporting licenses. Allan Steed, general manager of Lazzari's, describes the mesquite charcoal-making process:

> After the mesquite is felled it is either made into a pyramid or put into a pit dug in the earth. The size of the pyramid or pit varies greatly and will produce from two to fifty tons of charcoal at the end of the process. A large pyramid may stand ten feet tall and the thirty or more feet in diameter. The largest logs are placed in the center of the pile, with smaller and smaller pieces placed towards the outside. The fine network of outside branches is then covered with straw, burlap, and a layer of earth. Fire is then introduced to the inside of the earth-covered pyramid or pit and the wood allowed to smolder. As the mesquite wood smolders in the absence of oxygen it is slowly converted to charcoal. The process may last one or two days for a small amount to two or three weeks for a large quantity. The pyramid or pit must be watched constantly—twenty-four hours a day—while the mesquite smolders. As the wood settles, holes can occur in the dirt "shell," allowing oxygen to enter. The presence of oxygen would result in a full-fledged fire, reducing the mesquite to a pile of ashes rather than charcoal. All hands

... covered with straw, burlap and earth ...

are required to stand watch on these piles of mesquite—it's not unusual to see four-or five-year-old children standing guard—and, unfortunately, lapses in attention do occasionally occur, the result of which is quite a disaster.

The current and widespread popularity of mesquite has led, naturally, to the surfacing of opinions of the poo-pooers and nay-sayers. Those who dislike mesquite complain of its high heat and its characteristic aroma. I have cooked over mesquite for a number of years now and have found there are far greater advantages to the high heat than there are problems, and that it is a simple matter to get used to a fire that starts out hotter than a briquet fire. I've also found that mesquite charcoal stays hotter longer, a distinct advantage when grilling foods with a long cooking time, such as ribs or a roast. And I'd say that anyone who thought the aroma of mesquite overwhelmed some foods was simply full of monkey fur. The aroma of mesquite charcoal is very light and pleasant; I've yet to have anyone complain of it, and, in fact, very few ever even comment on it. This may not be the case with mesquite *wood* (not charcoal), which has a stronger aroma (see page 49).

If you're wondering whether the popularity of mesquite will result in its eventual disappearance, the answer is a qualified "maybe." Mesquite from Arizona and New Mexico is harvested from state-owned land, with no efforts to reforest. The fact that it is a hardy, fast-growing, and, in many areas, invasive tree is in mesquite's favor.

... and then allowed to smolder for up to three weeks.

The result: mesquite charcoal.

BEFORE YOU START
THE FIRE

Successful grilling revolves around two basic principles: (1) because it is such a straightforward manner of preparing food—food that is often unadorned with the masking qualities of complex sauces or seasonings—a commitment to the freshest, highest-quality ingredients is a must; and (2) in order to feel confident and comfortable with the process of cooking over direct heat, you will need to master the techniques on the following pages.

The worst thing that can happen is to overcook something. An undercooked whatever can always go back on the grill until the desired degree of doneness is achieved; when something is overcooked, about the only thing to be done is to chew and bear it, or call out for pizza. With that admonition in mind, let's get started.

WHERE TO PLACE THE COALS

Uncovered Grills

Placement of coals depends on the kind of grill you're using as well as the kind of food being cooked. Traditional grilling takes place by positioning the food directly over hot coals on an open grill. Grilling this way results in food with a crunchy, or slightly charred, exterior and a moist interior. Grilling directly over the coals is your only choice with an uncovered grill. And, as almost everyone knows, flare-ups are more the rule than the exception when using uncovered grills, especially with fatty foods.

Professional grill chefs use a technique for uncovered grills that can come in very handy for home chefs, as well. Instead of spreading the coals out in an even layer, the pros will often leave a portion of the coals close together—sort of "bunched up"—and spread the rest of the coals out evenly, with a little space in between them. By so doing, you have a grill with two different cooking temperatures: hot and hotter. This is particularly helpful if you have a large number of individual steaks, chops, chicken pieces, or even hamburgers. Use the hottest area of the grill to sear the juices in, and the cooler area for continued cooking. If any particular piece appears to be cooking too quickly or too slowly, you can simply rearrange the food on the grill to correct the matter. By arranging the coals this way you increase the flexibility of the grill by giving yourself two temperature options.

Covered Grills

The covered grill, in its many variations, gives the griller several choices:

1. Position the coals directly under the food and cook with the cover on;

2. Position the coals to the sides of the charcoal grill so that they are not directly under the food (a drip pan can be added, in this case, to catch juices), and cook with the top on;

3. Position the coals directly under the food, and cook without the cover on (although Weber, by far the largest manufacturer of covered grills, does not recommend this method).

Positioning the coals to the sides of a covered grill, or cooking "indirectly," is suggested for foods that take longer than 25 minutes to cook. This is sound advice, for it is difficult to turn something often enough during that length of time to prevent an overly charred exterior.

Although most manufacturers do not recommend using a covered grill without the cover, it can be done. This method does not take advantage of the design of a covered kettle-type grill, and problems arise from the fact that the grill and firebox are stationary. You have to have a pretty hot fire going to successfully cook something when the grill is 5 inches from the coals. (See pages 22–32 for further information regarding covered and uncovered grills.)

HOW MANY COALS?

The best way to gauge the number of coals needed is to imagine the approximate amount of space the food is going to take up on the grill and simply use enough coals to cover an equal area in the firebox, one layer thick, adding a few extra just to be safe. Covering the entire bottom of the firebox is a waste if all you are cooking is two New York steaks.

For indirect cooking (where the coals are not directly under the food) in a covered kettle, you will need enough briquets to form a row about 4 inches thick on each side of the food to be cooked.

WHEN ARE THE COALS READY?

Generally speaking, count on 30 to 40 minutes for the fire to reach the proper cooking temperature. Once the coals are well lighted, spread them out into an even layer. Although some professional chefs will often cook fish over a fire that is still glowing red, there is less chance of overcooking the fish, or what have you, if you wait until the coals are covered with a slight gray ash. At that point, hold your hand an inch or two over the grill. If you can't hold it there at all, the fire is still at the very hot stage. If you can hold it there for 2 or 3 seconds, the fire is hot. If you don't know how long 2 or 3 seconds is, do as my father taught me: spell M-I-S-S-I-S-S-I-P-P-I at a medium pace. If you can hold your hand directly over the grill and spell "Mississippi" at the same time, your coals are ready.

Generally speaking, there are three stages in a charcoal fire: *very hot:* when there are still flames licking around the coals; *hot:* when flames have died down, but coals are still bright red;

and *moderate* (for most foods): when the coals are just beginning to be covered with a light gray ash.

SAVING THE COALS

You can save your coals by closing the top and bottom air ducts on covered grills, or by spraying them lightly with water (after you've taken the food off) in an open grill. Mesquite charcoal can be saved up to three times this way, especially if the chunks were good-sized to begin with. Recycled coals take a little longer to get started than do fresh ones, and they don't burn quite as hot. For these reasons, it's best to use a combination of recycled and new charcoal each time you start a fire.

COOKING WITH SMOKE

I lied a little when I said there were only two fuels available for outdoor cooking: something new has been added, namely chunks of hardwood (*not* charcoal; these are like little pieces of firewood, if you will). These are being treated separately here because using chunks of hardwood and their smaller cousins, currently marketed as "smoking chips," constitutes, in my mind, a departure from traditional grilling—it introduces another element: aromatic smoke.

If you haven't already seen them, you soon will: bags of chunked, chipped, or shredded wood. The woods include apple, hickory, mesquite, oak, cherry, and maple—as well as corncobs. If your first thought on seeing these products is something like, "Now what am I supposed to do with these?" or, "This grilling business is getting entirely too complicated for me," take heart. You don't need them to produce a first-class feast; perhaps it's best to consider them as an option, like pin-striping or wire wheels on a car; they don't really improve the performance, they just add a little character.

If you want to try these products, you should know the following facts:

- Wood chunks do not burn as hot as chunks of charcoal.

- Wood chunks have greater aromatic qualities than does charcoal produced from the same wood. For example, fish cooked over a fire of mesquite wood chunks will have a more pronounced smoky flavor than fish cooked over mesquite charcoal.

- Hardwood chips or shreds are meant to be soaked in water before adding to the hot coals. When they are used, you not only get the aromatic quality of whatever type of wood you are using, but an attendant smoky flavor as well.

- Not all foods can stand up to the assertive qualities of these woods, particularly lean, delicate fish.

- Foods with more pronounced flavor, such as pork, lamb, oily fish, and game, are enhanced by the aromatic qualities of these woods.

- You'll get the fullest aromatic effect from these woods by using a covered grill. Obviously, with an open grill, much of the aroma and flavor is lost to the great out-of-doors (or to the great god Zeus, above).

- To get a long, slow release of smoke from hardwood chunks: wrap each chunk tightly in aluminum foil, then prick the foil all over with pinholes. Add the chunks to the hot fire, and they will release smoke through the holes for a long time.

Using Hardwood Chunks as Fuel

While specialty woods are meant primarily to be used dampened (added to an already hot charcoal fire), to impart an aromatic, smoky quality to your food, the hardwood chunks can also be used by themselves, in the place of charcoal (obviously, not dampened ahead of time).

If you are interested in using hardwood chunks as fuel by themselves, the procedure is quite simple. Start the fire by your preferred method, but, in this case especially, steer clear of lighter fluids. Wait for the coals to reach their desired temperature level (see page 47) and lay on your meal. Because the coals will not produce quite the intensity of heat as charcoal does, this is usually a slower cooking process, which allows more of the unique qualities of the wood to be imparted to the food. This is often the preferred procedure for cooking "barbecued" ribs, using hickory or mesquite chunks. (For a discussion of cooking over wood fires using logs as fuel, see Chapter Five.)

Using Aromatics with Charcoal

If an aromatic *and* smoky flavor is what you are after, try using the wood chips or shreds. Most of these products come with their own excellent instructions. What the instructions may not tell you is that there are basically two methods of smoking: cold and hot, each with its own unique results.

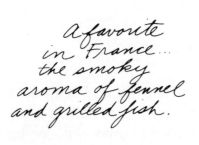

a favorite
in France...
the smoky
aroma of fennel
and grilled fish.

Hot smoking is slower than regular grilling, but faster than cold smoking. With hot smoking, you start with a hot bed of coals, then add the chips or shreds (which have been soaked in water for the recommended length of time, usually 10 or 15 minutes) to lightly cover the coals, and then put the cover on the grill. The smoke produced from the damp wood will envelop the food and produce a distinct flavor. Most cooks will partially close the top and bottom drafts to reduce the temperature, thereby lengthening the cooking time and intensifying the flavor produced. If you want to use this method, but only have the larger-sized chunks of wood, soak the chunks for 1 hour before putting them on top of the hot coals. Don't use too many soaked chunks or you may put the fire out; approximately one-quarter the total amount of regular coals is adequate.

Cold smoking is a long process best saved for a special event, or a Saturday when you have nothing else planned; a cold-smoked chicken or turkey can take up to 6 hours to prepare, with considerable attention from the chef. The idea is to keep just enough coals going in the covered grill (this demands a covered unit) to keep the temperature at approximately 140°F. Dampened chips or shreds of hardwood are added to keep the smoke continuously present, about every 20 to 30 minutes. A separate source of hot charcoal is necessary, as live coals must be added every 40 minutes or so to keep the temperature consistent.

Most cooks prefer to use a drip pan under the meat to catch any savory juices, poisitioning the coals on either side of the pan. With or without a drip pan, the coals should not be directly under the meat, but in two or more evenly spaced piles toward the outside edge of the charcoal grill. For most covered grills, two piles of 8 to 10 briquets (or similar-sized pieces of lump charcoal) will be enough to raise the temperature inside the covered grill to 140°F. Start with approximately 10 or more coals than are needed, then store the excess in a coffee can, or in a clay flower pot with a saucer underneath it. Add additional live coals when the temperature drops below 130°F. To keep the reserve supply going, add 4 to 6 pieces of fresh charcoal to the can or pot every 40 minutes.

As you can see, this process demands quite a bit of back-and-forthing, lifting off of the food and grill, and replenishing both the fuel and the source of the smoke, not to mention a watchful eye on the thermometer. (Note: if you have a Weber kettle, follow their instructions and line up the handles of the grill directly over the coals on either side of the drip pan. By doing so, you can add live coals and more smoking chips through the openings next to the handles, using a pair of tongs, without having to take off the grill or what's on it. This is a real convenience.) If you become a real fan of cold smoking, you might want to invest in a charcoal smoker, discussed on page 29 — it will simplify the process. The story would not be complete if I didn't tell you that the results of cold smoking can be outstanding, particularly when you relate the rigors involved in producing such sumptuous morsels to your admiring guests.

Easy aromatics can be achieved by simply throwing a handful of fresh aromatic leaves, stems, or cuttings directly on the coals

An old idea in a new package: grape cuttings for an aromatic grilled feast.

while the food is being grilled. Bay leaves, fruit-wood cuttings, herbs (woody perennial herbs seem to do best: rosemary, sage, tarragon, thyme), grapevine cuttings, even juniper twigs. This procedure adds a little aromatic quality as well as a slight smokiness. This is a very old technique, popular in many Mediterranean cultures. Using the homemade herb basting "brush" is another time-honored method of imparting the flavor of herbs to grilled foods. Simply tie a small bunch of fresh herbs together to form a small brush, and use for basting any food on the grill with melted butter or olive oil. In our modern culture, you should be sure not to use any stem cuttings or leaves of plants that have been recently sprayed with a pesticide or herbicide.

STARTING THE FIRE

A person from a more primitive culture would probably be astounded at the number of choices available to the modern American for the simple task of starting a fire; after all, starting a fire is what some people consider a basic, if not primal, skill. Starting a fire can be as simple or complex as you care to make it. Nonetheless, Americans have always been attracted to products that either save time, effort, or both, and so we have a number of alternatives in the marketplace.

The following methods will work for either charcoal briquets or lump charcoal; they are presented in historical order—that is, the order in which they became available to grillers.

Paper and Kindling

The old standby, paper and kindling is a satisfying way to start a charcoal fire, one that appeals to purists. Kindling, however, requires dry wood in manageable sizes and the ability to use a hand

Starting the fire for the evening meal is a ritualized event, charged with a sense of expectancy.

axe: for most people, those are two counts against it already. You can buy kindling, but it's very expensive for what it is. Otherwise, you will have to buy scrap lumber from a lumberyard and chop it yourself. But for those who approach grilling as a ritual, lighting the fire is an important, almost mystical step worth lingering over. Indeed, a basketful of uniform pieces of dry kindling and a neat stack of newspaper is a comforting sight for the person with the personality and time to appreciate such details.

Everyone I have ever witnessed using this method has developed a personal style, the perfection of which has been given considerable time and thought. As for handling the newspaper, there are "crumplers," "twisters," and "shredders." Kindling can be laid over the newspaper in "teepee" or "Indian" fashion, or in an architectural grid that forms a platform for the coals. Once the fire has been lit, the charcoal usually falls about, requiring a pair of long-handled tongs to place errant pieces back where they can be ignited by the burning kindling.

For ritualists there is a certain willful daring about this process. If the fire starts well and produces a bed of hot coals, there is an attendant feeling of smug assurance that the rest of the grilling procedure will go smoothly as well. If, on the other hand, the kindling fire dies out without successfully igniting the charcoal, it can set into motion a negative chain of events akin to getting out of bed on the wrong side in the morning. As I have said, there is an appeal in this challenge for a particular type of griller. However, if your life is already filled with enough challenges and the last thing you need is a defeat at this crucial stage of the game, I suggest trying another method, saving paper and kindling for a less stressful period in your life, say after retirement.

Lighter Fluid

If aliens from outer space landed in a typical suburban neighborhood around 6:00 P.M. on any given weekend, when the aroma of lighter fluid is at its most pervasive, they would surely conclude that ours is a volatile atmosphere. So ubiquitous is this odor that whole generations take one whiff of lighter fluid and immediately conjure up images of barbecued hamburgers, hot dogs, and playing outside until dark.

In its favor, lighter fluid is cheap and convenient, and it works every time. Stacking the charcoal into a neat pyramid shape is kind of fun, and the squirting on of the flammable juice brings out the most latent pyromaniacal tendencies in the best of us. A flick of a strike-anywhere kitchen match and WHOOOSH, we're off. Let's face it, this is a procedure that memories are made of.

As embedded in our collective consciousness as lighter fluid is, the environmental movement of the 1960s made us all more aware of the effects of chemicals on our environment and in our bodies. Like it or not, lighter fluid is on the wrong side of the fence when it comes to a "natural" approach to life, and, quite frankly, most professional chefs abhor its use.

Will lighter fluid survive another generation as the most popular way to announce the beginning of an outdoor feast? It's hard to say. But if those with the power to change our minds have their way, objections to its odor (in the air and in the food) and concern for the effects of petroleum by-products on our insides will probably win out, and the familiar red-capped squeeze can will become another artifact of a culture in transition.

The Electric Starter

This handy item appeared on the scene sometime in the 1950s, along with a rash of other New Age labor-saving devices such as the Hula-hoe and the dual-banded electric carving knife. The electric starter, basically a loop of electric element like those in electric ovens, has remained on the scene because it is a simple tool and it does what it is supposed to do. Because of its reliability and ease of use, most professional grill chefs use an electric starter to start the original charcoal fire, placing more charcoal at the edge of the bed of coals to add as the original coals begin to die down. Its only drawback is the necessity of a convenient electrical outlet. Other than that, it is a clean, relatively inexpensive, and very easy way to start a charcoal fire. For the longest life of the starter, you should keep your eye on the fire and not allow the element to "cook" in the coals any longer than necessary.

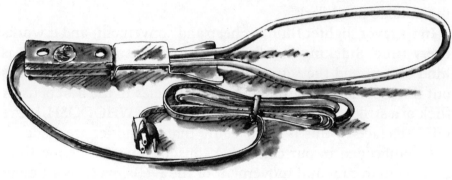

The electric starter is the first choice of many professional chefs.

The Metal Flue or Chimney

A newcomer with several points in its favor. This contraption, illustrated on page 57, is constructed of heavy sheet metal and is slightly larger at its base, with a wooden handle, several holes for ventilation at the bottom, and a rack near the bottom to hold the coals in place. Sound complicated? It's not. In fact, it is the simplest, cheapest, and most foolproof method for starting a charcoal fire that I have yet come across. Makers of the unit, which is sold under a variety of trade names including Easy Embers Charcoal Starter, claim that all you need to start the fire is a couple of sheets of crumpled newspaper (no lighter fluid is required) — which sounds like a challenge if there ever was one. Relying on the simple fact that hot air rises and will create a draft (or blast-furnace effect) in the proper circumstances, this thing (it really doesn't have a good generic name) makes a roar-

The metal chimney is probably the most foolproof method of starting charcoal without the aid of lighter fluid.

ing charcoal fire from the smallest glowing ember in 20 or 30 minutes, depending on the breeze. Its only drawback is that, I'm sure, a hole will eventually burn through its side or bottom, but by that time, after all it has done for the griller, it deserves to burn itself out. This unit could replace the tie as the traditional Father's Day gift in no time at all. It should be noted that you can make your own version of this product by taking both the top and bottom out of a large coffee can and poking holes around the bottom with a beer can opener. I have tried this method, and while it is satisfactory, it seems much easier to make the small investment in the real thing—complete with handle, heavy-gauge metal, and built-in draft device—rather than fool around with a homemade facsimile.

Starting Blocks

Again, here's a product in search of a good generic name. Under whatever brand they are sold (one brand name is Firestix), these small solid blocks, sticks, or rounds of compressed wood or paper product have been impregnated with a flammable substance, usually paraffin based. They should be placed at the base of a hand-stacked pyramid of charcoal. In their favor, there is little or no "off" odor or flavor imparted to the air or food, they can't spill, and they don't take up much room if you're hiking or otherwise going into the great outdoors where your fire-starting capabilities are going to be severely tested. In short, they work like a charm. Although no one has done a formal cost-comparison test on these units, my guess is that they are probably one of the more expensive ways to start a fire.

PRECAUTIONS

Make sure to keep your fire under control. While there is not much problem with charcoal briquets, mesquite charcoal is notorious for sending off sparks in the early stages of the fire. Look around you before you light the charcoal. Are there any places close by that are potential fire dangers? Dry grass, shingled roofs, and rain gutters filled with dry leaves or pine needles are a few of the things to watch out for. It's not a bad idea to keep an eye on the garden hose, just in case of an emergency. You should keep a container of water handy to douse flare-ups, if necessary, and have a pair of heatproof oven mitts ready to wear while turning foods. Most important of all: if you do use lighter fluid, *never* add fluid to a lighted fire or hot coals—fire can travel up the stream of liquid to your body. And be sure to keep kids from running or playing around a portable grill.

CHAPTER FOUR

A GRILLER'S GUIDE TO GOOD EATING

Those of you addicted to ritual probably already know the subtle pleasures of grilling outdoors in the same spot, at about the same time, on a regular basis. With whatever fortification you might need during that time of day when shadows start to lengthen, it can be particularly satisfying to take note of the pleasing little changes in your environment, such as the fact that the sliver of a moon that was right over the Monterey pines last week is, this week, over your shoulder, more than half full, or that the Japanese maple that was a tracery of bare twigs as you grilled fresh salmon in February is in lush leaf in the middle of

March (noticed while grilling a loin of pork, rubbed with olive oil and cracked pepper and studded with garlic). Grilling outdoors has the ability to connect us with the natural world. The pleasures of grilling can thus go far beyond that which is meant to be eaten. If the person approaching the grill is relaxed and receptive and not too goal-oriented, grilling can be a great way to end the day on a peaceful note, even in an urban environment.

When grilling is viewed as an experience rather than a chore, recipes and techniques seem less important. The simple fact is that as long as you don't overcook whatever it is you're grilling, you'll probably have a tasty meal and a good time preparing it. But for those of you who want to go beyond the standard dishes that have been the backbone of grilling for the last thirty years, we offer the following recipes, tips, and techniques, written and compiled by my co-author Jay Harlow, a professional grill chef, cooking teacher, and food writer. I have included some of my own favorite grilling recipes as well, and some recipes courtesy of my friend Ed Porter, chef at Norman's restaurant in Berkeley, California.

The recipes and menus presented on the following pages start where most other "barbecue" books and guides leave off. We assume that you are already familiar with hot dogs, hamburgers, steaks, and the ever-popular chicken "family pack." Which is not to say that there is anything wrong with these foods. To the contrary, if the old standbys weren't as satisfying as they always have been, charcoal grilling would have disappeared long ago. If you're in the mood for a little experimentation, however, and want to expand your culinary horizons to some fairly exotic tastes, we invite you to explore the following recipes.

This chapter is divided into the following sections: marinades and sauces, meat (beef, pork, lamb, veal, and variety meats), poultry (chicken, duck, squab, turkey), fish, shellfish, vegetables, and cheese and bread. A final section at the end of the chapter offers recipes for the perfect grilled chicken, ribs, steak, and hamburger from my fantasy of the perfect grill restaurant, Café Prometheus.

THE ESSENTIALS OF GOOD GRILLING

The following can serve as a checklist at first, but with time, all of these points will become second nature to the successful grill cook.

The Fire Start the fire well enough in advance (30 to 45 minutes), and be sure it is hot enough. If in doubt, build a bigger fire than you think you will need; nothing is more frustrating than trying to cook on a fire that is too cool. Arrange the burning coals with hotter and cooler parts if space allows, to give you more flexibility in where to place the food. Packing the coals together will give hotter spots, and spreading them out gives a cooler fire.

The Grill Keep the grill surface clean, oil it well while it is cold, and preheat it thoroughly. Skipping any of these steps is asking for trouble.

The Food Use the best possible ingredients. Have the food (especially meats and fish) at room temperature for faster cooking. Cut everything into manageable pieces, as uniform in size as possible.

The Tools Have everything you might need at hand—spatula, tongs, fork, basting brushes, etc.—so you won't have to leave the fire to dash into the kitchen for just the right tool. Have a table or some other working surface within reach for assembling plates.

The Timing Grilling can be a split-second cooking method, so try to keep the rest of the menu simple. Choose side dishes that can be prepared ahead of time and don't mind waiting for that moment when the fire is perfect.

The Cook Remember, this is supposed to be fun. Give yourself plenty of time, and don't worry if the fire dictates that you eat sooner or later than you planned. Have something around to munch on, your favorite preprandial beverage nearby, and relax and enjoy.

Please Note! Unlike ovens and stoves, with their more or less exact temperatures and similar characteristics, grilling is an inexact procedure filled with countless variables. Therefore all the grilling times in the following recipes should be used as rough guidelines only. When it comes to timing, experience, with your own set of variables, is definitely the best teacher.

HOW TO TELL WHEN IT'S DONE

One of the trickiest aspects of grilling is knowing when something is done. There are a number of different tests for different foods.

Peeking is probably the most primitive way to tell when something is done. One can take a peek inside the food either by piercing it with a long-handled fork or a metal or bamboo skewer or by cutting into it with a sharp knife. Using a knife is frowned upon because it destroys the contours of the food, and because valuable juices are lost in the process. Piercing and then peeking with a fork or skewer causes less juices to escape, but takes a little more skill and experience to judge the results. Here are the criteria:

For fish: The flesh should be opaque on the outside but slightly translucent at the very center.

For chicken: Juices from near the joints should run yellow with just a trace of pink when pierced with a fork or a skewer; meat near the bones should be opaque.

For steaks or chops: The center of the meat will show rare, medium rare, or well done, to your taste.

Sound and Smell These two sensory tests are the most subjective and the least reliable, but are nonetheless good indicators of what's happening. A general rule of thumb is, if the food isn't making any noise, it's probably not cooking. The aroma of cooked food is different from that of uncooked food, and with some experience you may be able to lift off the lid of a grill full of chicken, take a whiff, and say confidently, "Smells like it's done." Actually, the sound and smell tests should always be used in conjunction with another test, just to be sure that your subjective hunger isn't clouding a more objective assessment.

Feel The way a piece of food feels (that is, the way a piece of food feels when you press it with your finger) can be a strong indicator of the degree to which it is done. The method is used by many grill chefs, particularly for steaks and chops, and to a lesser degree, for cut-up chicken, particularly breast meat. It is also a good idea to press on a piece of uncooked meat to experience what a *really* rare steak feels like. With a little more experience you can graduate to using the bottom side of the tines of a long-handled fork in the same manner as your finger—a slightly more professional approach that won't require your guests to puzzle over what you're doing out there sticking your finger on all the steaks. To test fish for doneness by using a skewer, see page 128.

Time One of the best places to start is to have a rough estimate of how long it takes to cook a particular food and to use one or more of the above tests when you start nearing the end of the suggested cooking time. The main drawback of using the time method is that there are simply too many variables — distance of grill from fire, heat of fire, covered or uncovered grill, etc. — for it to be completely reliable. In all the recipes in this book we have suggested approximate cooking times.

Internal temperature can be read with a meat thermometer, but the use of such an instrument demands that there be enough mass for the thermometer probe to penetrate at least 1 inch, which makes this method impractical for many fish, steaks, chops, ribs, and the like. It does work well for large roasts, whole fowl (turkeys and large chickens), and the occasional very thick cut of beef or lamb, such as a Chateaubriand or butterflied leg of lamb. Some meat thermometers indicate degrees of doneness for various meats. In the table below we have reproduced those recommendations on the left. On the right we have listed temperatures that reflect more contemporary tastes. It is important to know that a good-sized roast of any type continues to cook after it has been removed from the grill. Experienced cooks have learned to take meats off the grill when they are 5 to 10 degrees *below* the desired temperature. Unless you like your foods on the well-done side, do not use the indications given on a meat thermometer as your guideline; use it as a temperature gauge only.

Meat	Standard Meat Thermometer	Contemporary Standards
Poultry	185	175–185
Lamb	175	140 (rare)
		160 (medium)
		170 (well done)
Pork, fresh	170	170
Veal	170	160–165
Beef, well done	170	up to 170
Beef, medium	160	140
Beef, rare	140	130–135
Ham, cooked	130	130

Marinades and Sauces

An important way to add flavor to grilled foods before, during, or after cooking is with a marinade or sauce. The distinctions between the two become a bit fuzzy at times, but basically a marinade is something applied to the food before cooking, and a sauce is something that is eaten as part of the dish. Understanding the working of marinades and sauces will add greatly to your grilling skill and your repertoire of grilled dishes.

MARINADES

Strickly speaking, a marinade is "a seasoned liquid, cooked or uncooked, in which foodstuffs, notably meat and fish, are steeped" (*Larousse Gastronomique*). The purpose of a marinade is to moisten and flavor the food, and in some cases to tenderize it.

The simplest form of marinating liquid is oil flavored with salt, pepper, and perhaps an herb or two. Because there is no acid liquid involved, this type of marinade has no tenderizing effect. However, many foods (including most fish) need no tenderizing; in fact, an acid ingredient would chemically "cook" delicate fish, turning it into *ceviche* before it hits the grill.

The purpose of this type of simple oil marinade is threefold: it moistens the surface of the fish, slowing down the evaporation of the natural juices during the cooking process; it spreads the flavors of the seasonings over the surface of the fish, and it helps to keep the fish from sticking to the grill. If only the last is important to you, a simple brushing of a neutral vegetable oil will do. If you want the marinade to provide more flavor, start with olive oil or another oil with a distinctive flavor.

While the simple oil and herb marinade is appropriate to delicate fish, some firmer fish and most meats will benefit from a marinade that penetrates the food. In general, this means a mildly acidic liquid: wine, citrus or other fruit juices, vinegar, or various soured milk products, including yogurt and buttermilk. The choice is often a matter of geography or climate. Not surprisingly, wine marinades are most common in temperate zones where wine is made. Throughout the alcohol-abstaining Moslem world, yogurt or fruit juices give acidity to marinades. In tropical and subtropical areas, citrus juices, pineapple, and tamarind are available and preferred.

Seasonings for marinades follow similar regional preferences. Ginger and soy sauce marinades are favored from Korea to Indonesia, with fermented fish sauce replacing soy sauce in much of Southeast Asia. Fresh or dried chilies appear in marinades throughout the tropics, in both the Old and New World. The favorite spice and herb mixtures of each region, from the elaborate spice blends of India and the Middle East, to the fragrant herbs of the Mediterranean and the chili-oregano-cumin pastes of Latin America, generally find their way into marinades for grilled foods.

It is not necessary to have all the food submerged in a marinade to flavor the food evenly. Just toss everything well in the marinade. If marinating for several hours or overnight, be sure to turn the food several times to expose all sides equally to the marinade, and to refrigerate the marinating food for all but the last half hour or so before cooking, to avoid spoilage. You will probably want to cover most marinating foods with plastic wrap.

Foods for grilling are sometimes seasoned just with dry ingredients, but left to season for a long enough time that the technique could be called "dry marinating." The grilled duck on page 118, derived from a standard Chinese preparation but using Western seasonings, is an example. During the long seasoning period, the salt draws some moisture out of the skin of the duck, which helps dissolve and spread the flavor of the other aromatics. Dry marinating is not recommended for most meats, however, as it can draw out too much moisture.

TANDOORI MARINADE
WITH YOGURT
For Chicken or Lamb

■ ■

Along with the explosion of mesquite-grill restaurants in this country has come a steady increase in Indian restaurants, both here and in England, featuring *tandoori* meats. Skewers of marinated meats and spitted whole chickens are cooked in the high heat of the *tandoor*, a top-loading earthenware oven fired by charcoal or wood, and acquire a delicious, almost crisp surface that seals in the juices of the meat.

While not many of us are likely to install tandoori ovens in our kitchens or backyards, by using similar marinades and cooking the meats directly over a charcoal fire we can get almost as good a result.

1 tablespoon chopped garlic

1 tablespoon chopped fresh ginger

4 tablespoons peanut or other vegetable oil

½ teaspoon garam masala*

½ teaspoon ground turmeric

⅛ teaspoon cayenne (or more to taste)

½ cup yogurt

½ teaspoon salt

Combine all ingredients and taste for seasoning, keeping in mind that the cayenne flavor will get stronger after an hour or so. Makes about ½ cup, enough for 1 chicken, 3 to 4 pounds chicken parts, or 3 to 4 pounds boneless lamb.

Note In either recipe, if the traditional deep-red color is desired, use *achiote* oil in place of the oil called for in the recipe: infuse 1 cup of vegetable oil with ¼ cup whole *annatto* seeds for a week or more.

*A variable Indian spice blend, used in a wide range of dishes. A typical mixture is 2 parts each black pepper, cardamom seeds, coriander seeds, and cumin, and 1 part each cinnamon and cloves. Freshly ground and tightly sealed in a jar, it will keep for a few months, but it is best made frequently.

TANDOORI MARINADE
WITH SAFFRON
For Chicken

■■■■■■■■■■■■■■■■■■■■■■■■

This recipe is adapted from Charmaine Solomon's Spiced Roast Chicken (Tandoori Murgh) in her *Complete Asian Cookbook* (New York: McGraw Hill, 1976). The saffron is an important ingredient, so don't skimp. If you really can't stand the cost of real saffron, you can substitute a whole *tablespoon* of Mexican safflower threads (available in Latin American groceries, often labeled *azafran*, which is Spanish for saffron). The flavor won't be quite the same, but it will still be good.

½ teaspoon saffron threads

2 tablespoons hot water

1 tablespoon minced garlic

1 tablespoon paprika

¼ teaspoon cayenne

½ teaspoon garam masala
(see footnote for preceding
recipe)

2 tablespoons tamarind water*
or lemon juice

½ teaspoon salt

2 tablespoons peanut or other
vegetable oil

Crumble the saffron threads into a small bowl, cover them with the hot water, and soak until the water is well colored, about 10 minutes or longer. In a blender or mortar, combine the saffron and water with all the remaining ingredients and blend to a smooth paste. Makes about ⅓ cup, enough for 1 frying chicken or 3 to 4 pounds chicken parts.

*Tamarind paste is the pulp of the seed pod of a tropical tree, available in small bricks in Asian groceries. Tamarind water is made by soaking the paste in warm water, then straining out the seeds and fibers. Use 1 teaspoon paste to ¼ cup water. It will keep for several weeks in the refrigerator.

SATAY MARINADE
For Beef or Pork

■ ■

Satay, like *tandoori*, is actually a technique rather than a flavor (all it actually means is "skewered and grilled"), but to most people it suggests the typical seasonings of Southeast Asia: ginger (or its relatives *galangal* and turmeric), coconut milk, fermented fish sauce, and tamarind. Satay marinades themselves are generally not too spicy or hot, because the meat is typically served with an intensely flavored peanut sauce or chili-flavored *sambal*. If you want to serve the meat alone, feel free to add more flavor to the marinade in the form of *garam masala*, black or white pepper, or cayenne.

2 teaspoons coriander seeds or ground coriander

1 teaspoon dried galangal flakes (or 2 or 3 slices) or 1 teaspoon ground galangal* (optional)

1 tablespoon chopped fresh ginger

1 tablespoon chopped garlic

2 tablespoons fish sauce**

2 tablespoons tamarind water (see footnote for preceding recipe)

If using whole coriander and galangal flakes, grind them to a powder in a spice grinder. Mince the ginger and garlic together until very fine, or, better still, pound them in a mortar to an almost liquid paste. Combine the ginger-garlic paste with the ground spices, fish sauce, and tamarind water in a bowl large enough to marinate the meat. Makes about ⅓ cup, enough for 1 to 1½ pounds of beef or pork.

*A rhizome related to ginger but with a more exotic aroma and taste. It is available in Asian groceries in small bags, either powdered or (preferably) in flakes. Sometimes called "laos" or "laos root." Powdered ginger plus a little turmeric is a vague substitute.

**The Southeast Asian counterpart of soy sauce, a salty brown extract of fermented anchovies. Thai, Vietnamese, and Philippine brands are available here in Asian groceries. Soy sauce is a not particularly good substitute.

SPICY INDONESIAN MARINADE

For Chicken or Turkey

■ ■

This combination of unusual ingredients makes an excellent marinade for chicken or turkey parts or brochettes.

6 to 8 garlic cloves, peeled

¼ cup chopped fresh ginger

2 tablespoons chopped coriander root (see page 80)

1 tablespoon dried galangal slices or flakes (see preceding recipe)

2 tablespoons tamarind water (see page 67), or juice and grated rind of 1 lemon

2 tablespoons fish sauce (see preceding recipe)

2 teaspoons roughly chopped dried shrimp or dry shrimp paste (available in Asian groceries)

½ teaspoon powdered chili

¼ cup unsweetened coconut milk*

Combine all the ingredients in a food processor or blender and blend until smooth. Makes about ¾ cup, or enough for 3 pounds cut-up poultry or 2 pounds brochettes.

*Canned unsweetened coconut milk (not the liquid from inside the coconut, but an extract made from the meat of the coconut) is available in Asian groceries. Most of it comes from Thailand or the Philippines.

Asian markets abound with specialty products with authentic flavors.

ADOBO

Chili-Spice Paste for Pork

■ ■

Both Mexico and the Philippines have many versions of *adobo*. In Mexico, it is mainly a seasoning paste for braised or stewed pork, usually with dried red chilies. In the Philippines, adobo is a whole genre of meat and poultry cookery, a family of highly seasoned stews. About all the two versions have in common is garlic, pepper in some form, and vinegar. A Mexican-style adobo also makes a delicious, though not especially authentic, marinade for grilled pork chops. Try it on chicken or turkey parts, but do not marinate these overnight.

4 to 6 ancho, New Mexico, or California dried chilies (ancho gives the fullest flavor, California the mildest)

½ teaspoon dried oregano

¼ teaspoon ground cumin

¼ teaspoon ground black pepper

3 garlic cloves, peeled

Juice of 1 orange, 1 lemon, and 1 lime

½ teaspoon salt

Remove the seeds and veins from the chilies, tear the chilies into small pieces, and soak them in warm water until they begin to swell, about 30 minutes. Drain, reserving the water. Combine all the ingredients in a blender or food processor and blend to a not-too-smooth texture (there should still be pieces of chili identifiable in the paste). If more liquid is needed to blend, add a little of the soaking liquid. Makes about 1 cup, enough for 6 to 8 chops or 2 pounds of cubed pork.

RECADO ROJO

For Fish, Poultry, and Pork

■■■■■■■■■■■■■■■■■■■■■■

This is a Yucatán-style seasoning paste for fish and meats (see Shark with Recado Rojo, page 140).

¼ cup achiote seeds or ground achiote paste*

1 teaspoon cumin seeds

1 teaspoon dried oregano

4 garlic cloves, peeled

½ teaspoon salt

⅛ teaspoon cayenne, or to taste

Juice of 1 lemon and 1 lime

Grind the *achiote* seeds, cumin, and oregano finely in a spice grinder. If using achiote paste, grind the cumin and oregano, then blend with the paste. In a mortar, pound the garlic with the salt and cayenne until it liquifies. Add the ground spices and pound to a paste. Combine the paste with the fruit juice in the mortar or in a separate bowl. Makes about ⅔ cup, enough for 4 servings of fish, poultry, or pork.

*Achiote (*annatto* seed) is available in Latin American and Philippine groceries and spice shops. Latin American shops carry cakes of ground achiote preseasoned with oregano and cumin.

Natural partners: grilled foods and garlic.

SAUCES

■▬■▬■▬■▬■▬■▬■▬■▬■▬■▬■▬■▬■▬■▬■▬■

Many grill aficionados will tell you that sauces are really unnecessary accompaniments to grilled foods: a simple cooking method should be simply presented. There is some merit in this philosophy. If you use excellent-quality ingredients, a sauce may indeed be unnecessary, but even purists will present fish with a little lemon, butter, paprika, or chopped parsley, or steak with a few mushrooms sautéed in butter and red wine.

We think a great sauce can make a great grilled food even better, and following are several different kinds of sauces to accompany the entire range of grilled foods. If you're going to learn how to make only one sauce, however, learn to make the *beurre blanc* on page 85. It's an outstanding sauce that has many simple and tasty variations. The fact that you can make it a couple of hours ahead of the dinner and keep it warm in a Thermos is a real boon; this also takes some of the panic out of its creation. If it doesn't turn out the first time, you can always try again without the last-minute threat of anxious, hungry diners looking over your shoulder as you silently pray to the god of emulsified sauces.

BASTING SAUCES

This category includes the familiar tomato-based "barbecue" sauces, as well as the Japanese teriyaki and yakitori sauces. Teriyaki sauce has now become a familiar item to most Americans, as most of the soy producers now offer a sweetened, ginger-flavored sauce right next to their soy sauce on the grocery shelves. What these two types of basting sauces have in common is that they should be applied only after the meat has been partially cooked; if applied sooner, the sauces will burn before the meat is done. This is especially true of fruit-based sauces or any that contain a quantity of sugar. To be on the safe side, plan on

Any basting sauce can (and should) be personalized to your own tastes.

basting with sweetened sauces only during the last 15 minutes of cooking a large cut of meat or poultry. (Of course, if all you are cooking is a salmon steak, teriyaki style, the sauce can be applied from the beginning.)

A problem arises when you want to marinate the meat before grilling. One solution is to prepare a similar mixture of flavors, but without the sugar—for example, just soy, sake, and grated ginger—for meat to be grilled and finished with teriyaki sauce. Another way is to thin some of the sauce with an appropriate liquid, such as wine or beer. In the latter case, wipe off any excess marinade before grilling to avoid any trace of a burnt-sauce flavor.

As mentioned elsewhere in this book, "barbecue" is really a separate world of wood-burning cookery, and one that many people have strong feelings about. We don't want to get drawn into the controversy over which part of the country has the best or most authentic barbecue. What we offer is a few recipes for barbecue sauces that taste good on pork, chicken, sausage, or beef.

PLUM-BASED
BARBECUE SAUCE

■ ■

This makes a "medium" sauce, one that has some chili flavor but not enough to send you racing for another beer. For a hotter sauce, add ½ teaspoon cayenne along with the mustard.

¾ cup Chinese plum sauce (Koon Chun brand, or another with red chilies — available in Chinese groceries)

1½ teaspoons dry mustard

½ teaspoon cayenne (optional)

½ bottle beer

Combine all the ingredients in a skillet or saucepan. Bring to a boil, reduce heat, and simmer until slightly thickened. If large pieces of fruit remain, strain them before using this as a basting sauce. Makes 1¼ cups, or enough for a 3-pound slab of spareribs.

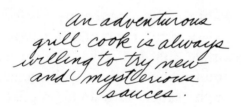

An adventurous grill cook is always willing to try new and mysterious sauces.

VARIATION Substitute bottled hoisin sauce (available in Chinese groceries) for the plum sauce in the above recipe, and use at least ¼ teaspoon cayenne. This sauce will not need straining.

TOMATO-BASED
BARBECUE SAUCE

■ ■

Commercially bottled barbecue sauces are based on tomatoes, but usually involve all sorts of questionable ingredients such as modified food starch, artificial smoke flavor, and so on. Even the so-called "all-natural" sauces use dehydrated onion and garlic. Imagine how a barbecue sauce made from fresh ingredients would taste! Here's a good basic recipe that you can adjust to your own taste.

2 tablespoons vegetable oil

1 large onion, chopped

3 large garlic cloves, peeled and smashed

2 tablespoons chopped fresh ginger

2 pounds ripe tomatoes, roughly chopped (if tasty fresh tomatoes are not available, use a 28-ounce can of crushed tomatoes with tomato purée)

1 teaspoon dried oregano, crumbled

4 California or New Mexico dried chilies, seeded and torn into pieces

1 cup cider or red wine vinegar

¼ cup honey or brown sugar

2 tablespoons soy sauce

Seeds from 3 cardamom pods

5 cloves

1 teaspoon coriander seeds

½ teaspoon fennel seeds

1-inch piece of cinnamon stick, crumbled

1 tablespoon mustard seeds

Heat the oil in a saucepan and gently sauté the onion, garlic, and ginger until the onion is translucent. Add the tomatoes, oregano, chili pieces, vinegar, honey, and soy sauce. Grind the whole spices to a powder in a spice grinder or mortar and add them to the sauce.

Simmer 2 hours or more, stirring frequently to prevent sticking, until the sauce thickens. Strain the sauce through a fine food

mill or sieve. Use immediately, refrigerate, or pack into steri-
lized jars for future use. Makes 1 quart, enough for 3 to 4 slabs of
ribs or 4 to 6 chickens.

Note This makes a mild sauce. For a hotter sauce, taste halfway through cooking and add cayenne to taste, beginning with
about ¼ teaspoon and letting the sauce cook a few minutes
before tasting.

Many cooks find a bottled sauce they like and then add "a little of this and a little of that" to personalize the taste.

COMPOUND BUTTERS

Compound butters are the simplest of the butter sauces: just
softened butter flavored with one or more ingredients and requiring no cooking. A dollop of this mixture is placed right on
top of the grilled food as it is served, or the butter can be used as
a dipping sauce on the side. The possible variations are almost
limitless. Just about any herb that can be served without cooking can be made into a compound butter: parsley, chervil, basil,
thyme, rosemary, sage, oregano, marjoram, and on and on. Shallots, garlic, onions, or chives are often used in these butters. A
small amount of liquid can also be incorporated into softened
butter, further expanding the possibilities.

The recipe for Herb-Shallot Butter below can serve as a master
recipe for the suggested variations that follow (see also the cilan-

tro butter on page 138). In making up your own variations, keep in mind that many flavors grow stronger as the butter sits, especially overnight. This can be an advantage in some cases, such as with chili-flavored butters, or a disadvantage in others: onions, garlic, and shallots can become unpleasantly strong after many hours. Freezing the butter delays this, so you can safely make up a log of any compound butter and store it tightly wrapped in the freezer, ready to cut off as much as you need for an instant sauce.

HERB-SHALLOT BUTTER

■ ■

4 tablespoons unsalted butter, softened

1 tablespoon chopped mild herbs (parsley, chervil, thyme, or a combination)

1½ teaspoons minced shallot

Zest of ¼ lemon, minced

Salt, pepper, and lemon juice to taste

Beat the butter to a smooth, fluffy consistency. Add the remaining ingredients and beat until thoroughly combined. Correct the seasoning and set aside for a few minutes to an hour or more for the flavors to blend. Taste and correct the seasoning, if necessary.

Place about 1 tablespoon of the butter on top of each serving of grilled steaks, fish, chicken breasts, or *paillards* just before serving, or serve in a small ramekin as a dipping sauce. For an extra touch, put the butter in a pastry bag with a star tip and pipe it onto the food in a swirl or rosette. Makes 4 tablespoons, enough for 4 servings.

VARIATIONS For 4 tablespoons of butter, use any of the following in place of the herbs and shallot and season to taste with salt and pepper:

Garlic-Basil Butter 1 or 2 garlic cloves, blanched, peeled, and minced with 1 tablespoon chopped fresh basil.

Chili Butter 1 teaspoon ground California, New Mexico, or *ancho* dried chili, 2 teaspoons grated orange zest, 1 to 2 tablespoons orange juice (California chili will give the mildest flavor, *chile ancho* the strongest; make this the day before for the deepest flavor).

Ginger-Lime Butter 1 teaspoon minced or grated fresh ginger, zest and juice of ½ lime.

Red Pepper Butter 1½ teaspoons red pepper purée (cut a seeded and deveined red bell pepper or fresh pimiento into strips, sauté until soft, and force through a sieve or food mill to strain out the skins).

DIPPING SAUCES

This is something of a catch-all category for liquid sauces that are best served in individual ramekins. Most of these are too thin to pour on top of foods without having them run onto the plate.

The simplest dipping sauce is also one of the most delicious: just soy sauce with a little grated ginger. This sauce can be used for any grilled fish, poultry, or meat that does not have too strong a marinade. More complicated versions are found throughout eastern Asia: Japanese versions may use *dashi* (the dried bonito that is the source of the best Japanese stock), green *wasabi* horseradish, or sesame oil; Korean sauces typically use garlic as well; and Southeast Asian dipping sauces such as the Thai *nam prik* usually involve fermented shrimp paste, tamarind, and dried chili.

The unique flavors of many ethnic foods rely on imported ingredients available at specialty markets.

THAI SWEET AND SOUR
DIPPING SAUCE

For Fish or Meats

■■■■■■■■■■■■■■■■■■■■■■■■

Here is an adaptation of *nam prik* using the less-aromatic fish sauce.

¼ cup minced shallots

¼ cup minced garlic

1 tablespoon dried red pepper flakes

1 tablespoon peanut oil

¼ cup fish sauce (see page 68)

1 tablespoon brown sugar or Chinese golden sugar

¼ cup tamarind water (see page 67)

2 scallions, minced

1 tablespoon chopped cilantro

In a small skillet, cook the shallots, garlic, and red pepper flakes in the oil until they begin to brown. Remove from the heat and set aside.

Combine the fish sauce, sugar, and tamarind water in a small saucepan. Bring to a boil, stirring to dissolve the sugar. When the sauce comes to a boil, remove from the heat and stir in the shallot-garlic mixture and the chopped scallions and cilantro.

Serve warm or at room temperature as a dipping sauce for grilled fish or meats. Makes about ¾ cup.

Is there such a thing as too much garlic?

THAI GREEN CHILI SAUCE

For Fish, Chicken, or Pork

■ ■

This recipe from Somchai Aksomboon, owner-chef of Siam Cuisine of Berkeley, originally appeared in *The California Seafood Cookbook* (Berkeley, California: Aris Books, 1983). Coriander root is a common Thai ingredient and has a slightly different flavor from the leaves. Short of growing our own coriander, the closest we can come here is to buy bunches of fresh coriander (cilantro) with as much root on them as possible, and make up the difference with chopped stems.

2 ounces fresh green chilies (serrano, jalapeño, etc.), seeded, deveined, and chopped

¼ cup distilled vinegar

2 tablespoons chopped coriander root

1 tablespoon chopped garlic

Salt to taste

Combine all the ingredients in a blender or food processor and blend to a smooth sauce. Serve chilled or at room temperature with mild fish, chicken, or pork. Makes about ½ cup.

PEANUT SAUCE WITH CHILIES

■ ■

A spicy peanut sauce is the traditional dipping sauce for beef, pork, or lamb *satay* in much of Southeast Asia. This version is more or less traditional, while the sauce with dried shrimp (see page 82) is less authentic but just as tasty. They don't have to be used just for satay; try them with grilled chicken breasts or paillards, or some of the meatier fish, such as swordfish or tuna. If you cannot get unsweetened coconut milk, use the more common sweetened version and eliminate the sugar in this recipe.

¼ cup peanut or other vegetable oil

1 cup chopped onion

¼ cup minced garlic

⅓ cup minced fresh ginger

8 to 10 small dried chilies, finely chopped (or 2 heaping tablespoon dried red pepper flakes)

6 tablespoons sugar

⅓ cup fish sauce (see page 68) or soy sauce

¼ cup tamarind water (see page 67) or 3 tablespoons cider vinegar

½ cup unsweetened coconut milk (see page 69)

1 cup crunchy peanut butter

¼ cup chopped cilantro

Cilantro for garnish

Heat the oil in a skillet (nonstick is handy) over moderate heat. Fry the onion, garlic, ginger, and chilies gently, adjusting the heat so the mixture sizzles but does not brown too quickly. Cook until the onion browns lightly, about 8 to 10 minutes.

Meanwhile, dissolve the sugar in the fish sauce and tamarind water. When the onion has browned, add the fish sauce mixture and coconut milk to the pan. Stir in the peanut butter and cook another 5 minutes, stirring frequently to keep the sauce from sticking.

Remove the pan from the heat and let the sauce cool enough to taste it. It should be pleasantly hot, but balanced by the sweetness of the sugar, the cooling coconut milk, and the tart flavor of tamarind. Adjust the seasonings accordingly.

Stir in the chopped cilantro and serve warm or at room temperature as a dipping sauce for grilled meats or poultry. Use cilantro to garnish the dish. Makes 1 ½ cups, or enough for 6 to 8 servings.

PEANUT SAUCE
WITH DRIED SHRIMP

■ ■

This unorthodox version of peanut sauce uses dried shrimp, which can be found in Oriental and Latin American markets. Don't be put off by the strong smell of the dried shrimp; it dissipates quickly in cooking.

¼ **cup peanut or other vegetable oil**

¼ **cup chopped garlic**

⅓ **cup chopped fresh ginger**

¼ **cup dried shrimp, coarsely chopped (up to ¼-inch pieces)**

¼ **cup sweetened shredded coconut**

¼ **cup tamarind water (see page 67) or lemon juice, or 3 tablespoons cider vinegar**

½ **teaspoon cayenne**

1 **cup chunky or smooth peanut butter**

¼ **cup chopped cilantro**

Cilantro for garnish

Heat the oil in a skillet (nonstick is handy) over moderate heat. Fry the garlic, ginger, and dried shrimp gently, adjusting the heat so the garlic and ginger sizzle but do not brown too quickly. When the garlic begins to color, after about 8 to 10 minutes, add the coconut and cook another 2 minutes. Add the tamarind water and stir in the cayenne and peanut butter. Cook, stirring frequently to prevent scorching, another 5 minutes.

Remove the pan from the heat and let the sauce cool enough to taste it. It should be pleasantly hot, but balanced by the sweetness of the coconut and the tart flavor of tamarind. Adjust the seasonings accordingly, adding a little sugar if necessary.

Stir in the chopped cilantro and serve warm or at room temperature as a dipping sauce for grilled meats and poultry. Makes 2 cups.

FRESH TOMATO SALSA

■ ■

This versatile Mexican sauce can be served with almost any grilled food and can be made hotter or milder according to your taste. For the mildest version, use the long green Anaheim chilies; for a hotter sauce, use (in order of increasing hotness) the yellow wax or green Fresno varieties, or the small green *chile serrano* or *chile jalapeño*. In any case, including the seeds and veins of the chilies will make the sauce hotter.

2 large tomatoes, peeled, seeded, and chopped

2 scallions (green and white parts), minced

1 or 2 serrano chilies, seeded, deveined, and minced (or 1 jalapeño or 1 of the larger types)

¼ cup cilantro, roughly chopped

Salt to taste

Combine all the ingredients in a stainless steel or glass bowl. For the best flavor, let the sauce rest for a half hour or so before serving to let the flavors marry. Fresh *salsa* does not keep well, so make only as much as you expect to use the same day. Makes about ¾ cup.

HOT BUTTER SAUCES

This is another category of sauce that is limited only by the cook's imagination. By melting butter in a skillet and adding herbs, aromatics, flavored liquids, or what have you, you can create a wide range of delicious sauces in minutes. Most of the compound butters earlier in this chapter can be prepared as hot sauces by heating the butter first, then adding the remaining ingredients, cooking only long enough to flavor the butter. An advantage of this technique is that you can use more garlic, shallots, or onions than most people will want to eat raw.

Hot butter sauces can be served directly on grilled fish or paillards of meat or poultry, but serving the sauces in ramekins as dipping sauces is a little neater and allows each person to use just as much as he or she wants.

You don't have to have a kitchen nearby to make hot butter sauces; just heat the butter in a small pan before you cook the fish or meat, and keep the sauce warm at the edge of the grill while the food cooks.

HOT BUTTER SAUCE

■ ■

The following ingredients can be used to flavor 4 tablespoons of butter, enough for 4 servings.

Garlic-Herb Butter 1 tablespoon chopped garlic, 1 tablespoon chopped fresh basil or other herbs, salt and pepper to taste

Anchovy Butter 1 tablespoon drained capers, 1 tablespoon chopped garlic, 2 to 3 chopped anchovy fillets, a little chopped parsley

Salsa Butter ¼ cup Fresh Tomato Salsa (page 83)

VARIATIONS Add one of any of the following ingredients: 1 or 2 small green chilies (*serrano* or *jalapeño*), seeded, deveined, and minced; 1 small scallion, minced; 1 teaspoon each minced fresh ginger and garlic; 1 tablespoon soy sauce or fish sauce (see page 68); 2 tablespoons dried shrimp, chopped (see page 82); ⅛ tablespoon cayenne; juice of ½ lemon.

EMULSIFIED SAUCES

While simple hot butter sauces almost always "break," or separate into butterfat and solids, there is another family of sauces in which the butter is emulsified. *Beurre blanc*, in which the emulsifying agent is a strongly acid reduction of shallots, wine, and vinegar or lemon juice, is an important member of this family, and one of the most delicious of all sauces for grilled foods.

BEURRE BLANC

■ ■

The reduction that is the essential ingredient of this sauce can be made ahead of time and in quantity; it will keep for weeks in the refrigerator. With a little practice, this sauce can be made in a pot on the grill.

¼ cup minced shallots

¼ cup dry white wine or dry vermouth

¼ cup fresh lemon juice or white wine vinegar

1 cup (2 sticks) unsalted butter, cut into small pieces

Combine the shallots, wine, and lemon juice. In a stainless steel, enameled, or other non-aluminum saucepan, bring the mixture to a boil and reduce until the liquid is nearly gone and the mixture begins to darken. Do not let the reduction scorch. Remove the pan from the heat and let the reduction cool slightly. Stir in a piece or two of butter and stir steadily until it melts. Return the pan to very gentle heat, add another piece of butter, stir, and continue adding the butter a bit at a time as the previous pieces melt.

The butter sauce should become a creamy yellow, and the butter should not separate. If the butter begins to break, the heat is too high. Remove the pan from the heat and beat until the butterfat is absorbed. Continue adding butter until it is all incorporated. Season to taste with a little salt and pepper if desired, although none is really necessary.

Beurre blanc can be kept warm near the edge of the fire (make sure it does not get hot, or it will separate), in a warm-water bath, or in a Thermos. Makes 1 cup.

Beurre Rosé Use red wine and red wine vinegar for the reduction, to make a pale-red *beurre rosé*.

Ginger-Lime Beurre Blanc Add ¼ cup minced fresh ginger to the reduction and use lime juice; add some grated lime zest to the finished sauce. (For another lime beurre blanc, see page 137.)

Herbed Beurre Blanc Chopped fresh herbs can be added to the finished sauce: dill for trout or salmon, basil or cilantro for fish with coconut-milk marinades, tarragon for chicken, etc.

Coriander–Lemon Grass Beurre Blanc Add ½ teaspoon ground coriander seed and 1 tablespoon minced fresh lemon grass to the reduction. Use on delicately flavored fish.

If you learn to make just one sauce, learn to make beurre blanc.

Meats

The first step in successfully grilling meats is to choose an appropriate cut, one that is tender enough to cook by direct heat and is cut into a shape that will cook at the right rate for your fire and equipment.

In general, the tenderest cuts of any animal come from the loin. This is the area that produces the most sought-after beef steaks, including filet mignon, New York strip, T-bone, and porterhouse. The equivalent section of lamb and pork produces the most tender chops.

The sirloin of beef, the part just to the rear of the loin, also produces tender steaks as well as some cuts ideal for brochettes. The sirloin portion of pork is generally sold as part of the loin, while that of lamb is sometimes left attached to the leg. In either case, the sirloin provides tender chops or meat for brochettes.

After the loin and the sirloin, the next best areas of the animal for tender cuts are the rib and leg portions. Rib steaks or chops are not quite as tender as those from the loin, but they have plenty of flavor and are a good choice for grilling. The leg section, known as the "round" in the case of beef and sometimes "fresh ham" in the case of pork, has several different muscles that vary in tenderness. The best of these make good steaks and brochettes, but the small muscle known as the "eye of round" in beef will remain tough no matter how carefully you grill it.

Like the leg, the shoulder (beef chuck, lamb shoulder, pork "butt" or "Boston butt") has both tender and tough cuts, which should be separated before grilling. The tender portions of these cuts can be flavorful and delicious when grilled, but as anyone knows who has tried to grill a whole chuck steak, some parts can be quite tough.

PRIMAL BEEF CUTS

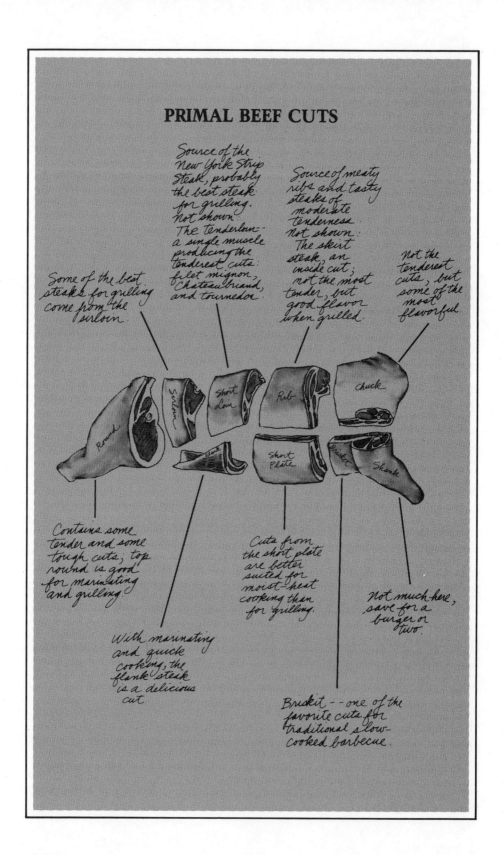

Source of the New York Strip Steak, probably the best steak for grilling. Not shown. The Tenderloin—a single muscle producing the tenderest cuts: filet mignon, Chateaubriand, and tournedos.

Source of meaty ribs and tasty steaks of moderate tenderness. Not shown. The skirt steak, an inside cut; not the most tender, but good flavor when grilled.

Not the tenderest cuts, but some of the most flavorful.

Some of the best steaks for grilling come from the sirloin.

Contains some tender and some tough cuts; top round is good for marinating and grilling.

Cuts from the short plate are better suited for moist-heat cooking than for grilling.

Not much here, save for a burger or two.

With marinating and quick cooking, the flank steak is a delicious cut.

Brisket — one of the favorite cuts for traditional slow-cooked barbecue.

RECOMMENDED MEAT CUTS
FOR GRILLING
Listed in Order of Preference Within Each Category

Beef

Steaks: New York strip (aka Kansas City strip, top loin), porterhouse, T-bone, club, filet, top sirloin, other sirloin cuts, rib, rib eye, flatiron, cross rib, top round, sirloin tip, rump, skirt, flank

Brochettes: sirloin tip, flatiron, top round, bottom sirloin, cross rib, rump, heart

Paillards: top round, top sirloin, rump

Miscellaneous: ribs

Spit-roasting: whole filet

Pork

Chops: loin (center, sirloin end, "blade" or rib end), shoulder steaks

Brochettes: shoulder, picnic

Paillards: loin, leg (fresh ham)

Spit-roasting: loin (bone-in or boned), boned shoulder, boned picnic

Miscellaneous: spareribs, "country-style spareribs"

Ground: shoulder, picnic

Lamb

Chops: loin, rib, shoulder

Brochettes: leg, shoulder, kidneys

Spit-roasted: boned shoulder, boned leg

Miscellaneous: butterflied leg, whole rib (rack), breast

Ground: shoulder

Veal

Chops: loin (porterhouse)

Spit-roasted: boned shoulder

Miscellaneous: liver, sweetbreads, breast

THE BEST CUTS FOR GRILLING

The general cuts of meat of interest to grill cooks are steaks and chops, paillards (sometimes called scallops or escalopes), brochettes (sometimes called kebobs), and ground meat in various forms, including sausages. These cuts alone can keep most cooks and guests happy for a lifetime of grilling, but there are plenty of other cuts that are excellent as well (see the preceding chart). For a full-scale discussion of meat cuts and useful tips on cutting your own meats from large cuts ("primal" and "subprimal," as they are technically known), see *Cutting Up in the Kitchen*, by Merle Ellis (San Francisco: Chronicle Books, 1975).

Steaks and chops are essentially equivalent cuts, with steaks usually referring to larger pieces and chops to those from smaller animals. Most beef steaks have their exact equivalents in other animals; for example, chops from the sirloin end of a pork or lamb loin contain exactly the same muscles as porterhouse steak, while those closer to the rib end look like miniature T-bone steaks.

What all these cuts have in common is that they are crosswise cuts of relatively large, tender muscles. They can all be grilled to perfection, especially if they are cut to the appropriate thickness. For *beef steaks*, this can be anywhere from ¾ inch to 2 inches thick, depending on the tenderness of the steak and the desired degree of doneness. The most tender cuts can be cut thicker, but the less tender ones are more successfully grilled (and eaten) if they are cut on the thinner side. Thinner steaks are also much easier to cook beyond the "medium" stage, if that is your preference.

Lamb chops from the loin or rib can be cut up to 1½ inches thick, ideal for serving medium rare, or left in large sections that are actually miniature roasts. Richard Olney, in his *Simple French Food*, (New York: Athenaeum, 1980) shows an excellent procedure for the latter: he leaves the "tail" or "apron" (actually a bit of the flank) attached and wraps it all the way around the smaller filet, securing it with a rosemary twig (see illustration). The apron protects the filet from overcooking while the chop is grilled on both sides, both ends, and the bone side.

Lamb chop à la Olney: wrapped in its own tail and skewered with rosemary.

Pork chops are usually cut somewhat thinner than lamb chops so they can be cooked well done, but a thicker chop cooked just to the point that it loses its pinkness in the center will be much juicier.

Paillards, scallops, escalopes, and cutlets are various names for similar cuts of boneless meats that may or may not be pounded before cooking. These may be cuts of the same muscles as steaks and chops (for example, the large muscle of a pork loin) or of other, less tender cuts. When pounded (or flattened) either a little or a lot, these can be useful in many ways: because they are cut very thinly across the grain, tougher cuts can be made to seem more tender. Thin slices also offer the maximum surface area for marinades. Busy restaurants find them especially convenient because they cook almost instantly, tying up the grill and the cook for a minimum of time. Split-second timing, however, is necessary to prevent overcooking and drying out. But if you cook them quickly and carefully, paillards can be an important addition to your grill repertoire.

Brochettes are not really cuts of meat. *Brochette* is the French word for skewers. The Turkish name kebabs, or kabobs, is probably a more accurate term for pieces of boneless meat cooked on skewers. Whatever you call it, grilling *en brochette* is a useful way to cook tender cuts of meat from smaller or oddly shaped muscles that do not cut easily into steaks. It is also a way to reduce a large cut of meat, such as a leg of lamb, to pieces that can be easily managed on an outdoor grill.

The size of the cubes can vary according to the same principle as steaks and paillards: more tender cuts can be cooked in thicker pieces, while less tender pieces should be cut across the grain into thinner pieces. Sirloin of beef, lamb, or pork, for example, can be cooked in cubes of an inch or two, but top round should be cut smaller, and bottom round or chuck should be cut into slices of not more than ½ inch thick. Cooking times will, of course, vary according to the thickness of the cubes.

Ground meat can be cooked in other ways than the obvious hamburgers. In the Middle East and across southern Asia, seasoned ground meats, sometimes bound with bread crumbs, are molded onto skewers for grilling, or formed into meatballs, which are then skewered. Sausages of various shapes can be grilled, either stuffed in the familiar casings or formed into patties with or without an encasing layer of caul fat.

Variety meats of most types are adaptable to grilling as well. Beef or calves' liver is excellent simply sliced and grilled; smaller livers such as chicken and rabbit are usually grilled whole, often *en brochette.* Kidneys of young animals, especially lamb, are sometimes included with the loin chops, or they may be cooked separately. Veal sweetbreads require a bit of preparation—blanching and removal of most of the membrane—but skewering them interwoven with a strip of blanched bacon and grilling them briefly makes it worth the effort. No sauce is necessary—just squeeze a little lemon juice over the brochettes as they come off the grill. Hearts of lamb, veal, and pork are tender enough for grilling without long marinating, and small cubes of beef hearts marinated in orange juice, chili, and cumin are grilled in Peru as a popular street and bullfight snack called *anticuchos.*

CARNE ASADA

Mexican Grilled Beef

■ ■

This is the Mexican version of a beef paillard—thin slices of meat grilled for just moments on a side. Most Mexican recipes call for skirt steak, and this is also the most popular cut for *carne asada* in *taquerías* in this country. However, several other cuts, including top round, sirloin, and rump, are also good.

1 pound beef steak or roast
(see list of cuts above), sliced
¼ inch thick across the grain

Salt and pepper to taste

Juice of 1 lime

With the side of a heavy cleaver or a meat pounder, pound each slice of meat to a little more than half its original thickness. (If the meat falls apart, you are pounding it too thin.) Season the meat with salt, pepper, and lime juice.

Grill over a very hot fire just until drops of blood appear on the top surface of the meat; turn and cook a few seconds for rare, a few seconds more for medium rare, a few seconds more for medium, and so on.

Serve on a plate with Fresh Tomato Salsa (page 83) and a serving of guacamole. Serves 2 to 3.

CARNE ASADA TACOS

■ ■

Prepare Carne Asada, preceding. Have ready a pile of warm soft corn tortillas, some fresh salsa, and if you like, some cooked and well-drained pinto beans. Chop the steak into bite-sized pieces and fold it into a tortilla with salsa and beans, to be eaten with the fingers. Be sure to provide plenty of napkins! A pound of beef will make enough for 6 to 8 tacos.

MARINATED FLANK STEAK
AND GRILLED MUSHROOMS

■ ■

By itself, the flank steak is a tough customer. A flavorful marinade, charcoal grilling, and cutting in thin slices at a 45-degree angle, however, make it into a real crowd pleaser. If there's any left over, cold flank steak sandwiches are hard to beat.

¼ cup vegetable or olive oil

¼ cup soy sauce

½ cup dry red wine

2 garlic cloves

1 small onion, minced

1½ teaspoons ground ginger

1 teaspoon coarsely ground black pepper

1 flank steak (1½ to 2 pounds)

1 pound medium-sized fresh mushrooms

Combine the first 7 ingredients in a blender or food processor and purée for 20 seconds. Lacking either apparatus, mince the garlic together with the onion; combine the other ingredients in a bowl and whisk until well mixed.

Marinate the flank steak in the refrigerator for 6 to 8 hours; remove from the refrigerator about 30 minutes before grilling. Just prior to grilling time, gently wash and skewer the mushrooms through the stems and caps. Prepare a hot charcoal fire and grill the flank steak for 2 turns, approximately 5 to 7 minutes each for rare and medium rare, respectively. Put the mushrooms on at the same time as the steak, but keep them towards the cooler edges of the fire. Slice the steak thinly at a 45-degree angle. Toss the mushrooms in the juices from the cutting board briefly before serving. Serves 4.

GRILLED RACK OF LAMB

■ ■

Butchers have different ways of preparing the whole rib, or rack, of lamb. Some racks contain 6 ribs, others 8. Specialty butchers often prepare the rack "French style" by removing all the meat and fat from the last inch or two of the rib bones. Supermarket meat counters are likely to carry the same size of rack with less trimming at a considerably lower price; you can trim it or not as you like. In either case, have the butcher cut through the backbone between the ribs to make carving easier. However you choose to buy the rack, allow anywhere from 2 to 4 ribs per person, depending on your appetite and the rest of the menu.

1 rack of lamb (8 ribs), about 2¼ pounds	**½ teaspoon coarsely ground black pepper**
Fresh rosemary or thyme	**½ bay leaf, crumbled**
1 teaspoon coarse kosher salt	

Trim the fat layer on the outside of the rack to ¼ inch or less. Insert small sprigs of rosemary or thyme into the cuts between the ribs and in any seams in the fat. Combine the salt, pepper, and bay leaf and rub the mixture all over the meat and fat.

Grill over a moderate fire in a covered grill or on an open grill, starting with the fat side but doing most of the cooking from the bone side, until the meat reaches an internal temperature of 140°F for medium rare, about 24 to 30 minutes. Grilled Potato Wedges (page 159) are a good accompaniment. Serves 2 to 4.

BREAST OF LAMB
WITH MOROCCAN MARINADE

■ ■

This recipe uses a dry spice mixture as a "marinade."

1 tablespoon minced garlic	½ teaspoon salt, or to taste
1 tablespoon ground coriander	1 breast of lamb, about
2 teaspoons ground cumin	1½ pounds
1 teaspoon paprika	Melted butter (optional)

Combine the garlic, coriander, cumin, paprika, and salt and rub the mixture over the surface of the lamb. Marinate 15 minutes or more.

Build a moderate fire on one side of a kettle grill. Sear both sides of the breast over the hottest part of the fire, cooking about 5 minutes on a side. Move the breast to the other side of the grill, positioning it as close as possible to the fire but not so close that the drippings flame. Cover the kettle and cook until done, about 30 more minutes. Turn the meat every 10 minutes, turning a new side toward the fire each time and basting with a little melted butter, if desired. The finished meat should be medium cooked, with a crisp layer of fat on the outside. Serves 3 to 4.

For people who love food, a trip to a new market can be an enlightening experience— filled with surprises and unexpected tastes.

TANDOORI LAMB

■■■■■■■■■■■■■■■■■■■■■■■■■■

Prepare Tandoori Marinade with Yogurt, page 66. Marinate 1½ pounds boneless lamb, cut into 1-inch cubes, in the mixture for several hours or overnight in the refrigerator. Remove the meat from the refrigerator at least a half hour before grilling.

Skewer the cubes of lamb and grill over a moderate fire to the desired degree of doneness, about 8 minutes for medium rare. Serve with rice and a fresh-vegetable relish such as cucumbers and tomatoes with fresh mint. Serves 4.

SKEWERED MINCED LAMB

■■■■■■■■■■■■■■■■■■■■■■■■■■

One of the commonest forms of grilled meat in much of the Moslem world is minced or ground lamb, seasoned, kneaded to a smooth consistency, and molded around skewers in a sort of sausage shape. Each region has its distinctive flavorings, from the fresh ginger and *garam masala* of India to the intricate mixture of dried spices known in Morocco as *ras el hanout*. This version leans toward the Indian style and is delicious served with a cool yogurt and cucumber relish.

If you want to be really authentic, you can chop the meat by hand. However, a food processor does the job quickly and very well. Ground meat will need still more chopping and kneading or a second grinding to achieve the right texture.

1 medium onion, peeled

2 garlic cloves, peeled

1 tablespoon chopped fresh
  ginger

3 or 4 cilantro or parsley sprigs

1½ pounds lamb shoulder
  (3 or 4 shoulder chops)

1 teaspoon salt

½ teaspoon ground cumin

½ teaspoon garam masala
  (see page 66)

Ground black pepper to taste

Combine the onion, garlic, ginger, and cilantro in a food processor and chop finely, or mince with a chef's knife. Cut the meat into cubes of an inch or so, discarding any large chunks of fat but leaving about 10 percent of the fat attached. If you are using shoulder chops with an arm bone, push out the marrow and add it to the meat. Add the meat, salt, cumin, garam masala, and pepper to the processor and chop the meat finely; process until the mixture begins to form a ball around the blade and the fat smears the sides of the bowl (or chop by hand with a chef's knife, or put through a meat grinder twice). Check the seasoning by tasting a bit of the raw mixture or a small amount that has been sautéed in a skillet, and adjust as needed.

With hands dipped in cold water, form the meat into 12 small cylinders, each molded around a short skewer. Pack the meat firmly onto the skewers to prevent its falling apart on the grill. Chill the skewered meat until about 15 minutes before grilling (skewers may be made up several hours in advance).

Grill over a moderate to hot fire to the desired degree of doneness, about 7 minutes for medium rare. Try to leave the meat in place for at least 4 or 5 minutes before turning; if moved too soon, it is likely to stick. Serve on the skewers, sliding the meat off onto plates or onto soft pita or Indian-style breads. Serves 4.

BUTTERFLIED
LEG OF LAMB

■ ■

A butterflied leg of lamb is unquestionably one of the most outstanding foods to come off a charcoal grill. A large leg, 6 to 7 pounds, will feed approximately 8 people, making it, if not economical, at least affordable—a perfect choice for a gathering of good friends.

Butterflying a leg of lamb takes time and effort. For this reason, it's a good idea to give your butcher a break and call in the order ahead of time. The resulting piece of meat will be somewhat uneven in thickness. Some cooks prefer to leave it uneven, assuming that some of their guests will prefer their lamb slightly more done than others; others use a mallet to pound it to a more even thickness. Without resorting to physical force, even those who have never had lamb cooked medium rare should be coerced into giving it a try. Serve this with grilled tomatoes and Potatoes Chevalier (page 163) and you've got quite a feast.

1 tablespoon each black, green, and white peppercorns (you can use canned or dried green peppercorns)

4 to 6 garlic cloves

½ cup olive oil

¾ cup dry red wine

1 large leg of lamb, about 6 to 7 pounds, butterflied

Coarsely grind the peppercorns in a mortar, blender, or food processor, or put in a cloth and pound with a hammer. Flatten the garlic cloves with the side of a wide knife; peel off the skins and chop the garlic roughly. Combine the liquid ingredients and add the garlic and peppercorns. Whisk well, or process for 20 seconds in a blender or food processor.

Marinate the lamb for 6 to 8 hours in the refrigerator, turning 3 or 4 times to distribute the marinade evenly; remove from the refrigerator about an hour before grilling.

Grill the lamb over a good-sized hot fire. Turn the lamb 4 times, 10 to 15 minutes per side—a total cooking time of between 40 and 60 minutes—for medium rare to medium well respectively. This is one case where you shouldn't be afraid to actually cut into the meat to check its progress. Cut in thin slices and serve with the juices that collect on the cutting board. Delicious with a big Zinfandel or Charbono. Serves 8.

Garlic and lamb: one of the all-time great flavor combinations.

SOUVLAKI PITA

Spit-Roasted Lamb Wrapped in Pita Bread

■ ■

Souvlaki pita is a popular street food in Greece, much like tacos in Mexican cities and hot dogs in America. In one popular form, slices of lamb or pork are stacked on a vertical spit and roasted in front of a vertical heat source. As the meat cooks, the souvlaki vendor slices off the outer half inch or so, exposing the less-cooked meat underneath. The meat comes off in small chunks, which are then wrapped in hot pita bread and garnished with a few pieces of tomato and a dollop of yogurt. The whole thing is wrapped in a sheet of waxed paper, making it a perfect carry-away snack.

This procedure starts with a whole shoulder of lamb, which is much more than you need for this recipe, but it gives you plenty of choice pieces to stack on the spit. The rest can go into your favorite lamb stew, or be ground and seasoned to make meatballs or patties, which can be cooked on the grill the next day. This may not be the authentic way to assemble the meat for souvlaki pita, but it works!

1 lamb shoulder, 4 to 6 pounds, boned

1 cup red wine

¼ cup olive oil

1 onion, sliced

1 bay leaf

½ teaspoon each dried thyme, rosemary, and oregano

1 teaspoon black peppercorns, cracked

1½ pounds tomatoes, peeled, seeded, chopped, and drained

2 cups thick yogurt

12 warm pita breads

Lay the boned lamb shoulder fat side down on the cutting board. Using your fingers and a boning knife, separate the meat along the natural seams into individual muscles. Trim the membranes and fat from each muscle. Select the largest, flattest muscles — enough to make 2 to 3 pounds — and set aside the rest for another use. The object is to assemble a stack of pieces, each

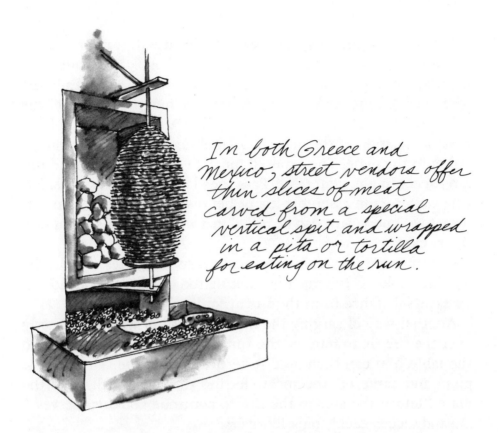

In both Greece and Mexico, street vendors offer thin slices of meat carved from a special vertical spit and wrapped in a pita or tortilla for eating on the run.

about ½ inch thick and 4 inches across. Thicker pieces will need to be butterflied, that is, cut *along* (not across) the grain almost through to one edge, then unfolded to an overall thickness of ½ inch or less. Combine the wine, oil, onion, bay leaf, herbs, and pepper and marinate the lamb several hours or overnight in the refrigerator.

An hour or so before cooking, assemble the meat on the spit as follows: attach the fork to the spit 4 to 6 inches from the center. Starting with a good-sized piece of meat, thread the meat onto the skewer, passing the skewer through the middle of each piece. Keep adding pieces of meat, pressing firmly against the fork to form a rough cylinder, with the grain of meat always running perpendicular to the skewer. Alternate smaller and larger pieces, but save a few large pieces to anchor the other end. When all of the meat is in place, attach the other fork, pressing it in well to compress the meat into a tight form. Don't worry if the edges look raggedy; the first few cuts will remove all the odds and ends. Let the meat drain its excess marinade over the bowl until the fire is ready for cooking.

Position the spit over the fire so the meat will turn an inch or two above the fire, turn on the motor, and cook 10 minutes, or until the outermost bits of meat begin to brown. Have ready the tomatoes, yogurt, and warm pita bread. When the outside of the meat looks nicely browned, hold a plate under the edge of the roast and carve off the outside ½ inch or so, letting the pieces fall onto the plate. The exposed meat should be rare to medium rare, according to your taste. Pass the plate around the table, letting each person assemble his or her own sandwich. The meat, tomatoes, and yogurt can be rolled in a whole pita or stuffed into the pocket.

Continue carving off bits or meat every 5 minutes or so as the outside cooks. If the meat is cooking too quickly or too slowly, adjust its distance from the fire accordingly.

Another way of carving the meat, instead of working directly over the fire, is to remove the spit from the fire and bring it to the table. You can then hold it vertically over the center of the plate and carve off the meat, letting the pieces fall onto the plate. Return the spit to the fire to continue cooking. Serves 6 (2 sandwiches each), plus leftovers.

TACOS AL PASTOR

■ ■

There is an almost exact equivalent of *souvlaki pita* (preceding) in some *taquerías*, in both America and Mexico, known as *tacos al pastor* ("shepherd style"). Slices of pork shoulder are skewered in the same way and roasted on a vertical spit, then carved off in small chunks to be folded into warm tortillas and garnished with fresh *salsa*.

Try tacos al pastor with plain, unmarinated pork or, just before skewering, season the slices with salt, pepper, and lime juice. You could also marinate the slices overnight in Adobo (page 70) or Recado Rojo (page 71). Serve with warm corn tortillas to make tacos, or use flour tortillas to make burritos.

PORK LOIN WITH WILD MUSHROOMS AND MADEIRA SAUCE

■ ■

This is a full-flavored meal, great for an early fall supper. Serve with Grilled Potato Wedges (page 159) and a green vegetable.

¼ cup olive oil

1 teaspoon minced fresh rosemary

2 garlic cloves, minced or pressed

One 1-pound pork tenderloin, cut into ¼-inch slices (approximately 3 or 4 per person)

1 cup chanterelles, sliced

1 cup shiitake mushrooms

3½ tablespoons butter

2 cups Madeira

Salt and pepper

Mix the olive oil, rosemary, and garlic in a stainless steel or glass bowl. Marinate the pork slices in this mixture for 4 to 6 hours, covered, in the refrigerator.

In a saucepan, sauté the chanterelles and *shiitake* mushrooms in 2 tablespoons of the butter until limp. Add the Madeira and reduce the mixture to approximately 1 cup while stirring constantly over high heat. Whisk in the remaining 1½ tablespoons of butter and season to taste. Keep warm until ready to serve.

Grill the pork slices over a hot fire. Do not turn them until you see drops of blood surfacing on the side away from the fire. Turn immediately, and cook for approximately the same amount of time on the other side. This is a very fast procedure, taking probably no more than 3 or 4 minutes. Overlap the pork slices on hot plates and ladle on the sauce, with equal amounts of mushrooms for each serving. Serves 4.

Courtesy of Norman's restaurant, Berkeley, California.

PORK CHOPS IN ADOBO

■ ■

Spread ½ cup Adobo, page 70, over four 1-inch-thick pork chops and rub it in well on both sides of the meat. Marinate overnight in the refrigerator. Remove the meat from the refrigerator a half hour before cooking.

Grill over a moderate fire until the juices run clear near the bone when pierced with a fork or skewer and the meat springs back when pressed, about 12 to 15 minutes. Serve garnished with cilantro. Grilled Cheese-Stuffed Peppers (page 156) are a good accompaniment. Serves 4.

SATAY PORK

■ ■

Prepare Satay Marinade, page 68. For 1 pound boneless pork shoulder or loin, cut into ½-inch cubes, toss the meat in the mixture, and let it marinate at least an hour or, preferably, several hours in the refrigerator.

Remove the meat from the refrigerator at least a half hour before cooking. Thread the meat onto skewers and grill over a hot fire until just done but still moist, about 5 minutes. Serve with a peanut sauce (see pages 80–82) and rice. Serves 6 to 8 as an appetizer, 3 to 4 as a main course.

PORK OR CHICKEN
SPICY KEBABS

■ ■

Spicy Kebabs are somewhere between Japanese teriyaki and Southeast Asian *satays*. They have several good things going for them: they are the perfect meal for 2 people; because they feature lean cuts of meat, they are low in calories and high in protein; they need nothing larger than a small hibachi and a dozen or so hot coals to cook them; they cook in no time at all; and they are very satisfying, especially for those who like spicy foods. (They are also excellent as hors d'oeuvres.) The main drawback is that they require a little advance preparation—they should be marinated from midday on for the evening meal. Reducing the leftover marinade over high heat will produce an intensely flavored dipping sauce (if there's not much marinade left over, add additional liquid of your choice—such as chicken broth, water, or wine and water—before reducing). The only accompaniments needed are some steamed rice and perhaps a few stir-fried vegetables and a bottle of beer or two.

Thin pork chops (cut away from the bone and trimmed of fat) and boned and skinned chicken breasts seem to be the best cuts for pork or chicken kebabs. For some reason, they taste best when the meat is cut into 1-inch-wide strips rather than chunks. For 2 people, 1 pound of pork chops (depending on thickness and hunger), or 1 whole, large chicken breast (2 halves) should suffice. Have the rice, vegetables, cold beer, and the dipping sauce made from the reduced marinade all ready to go by the time you put the skewered meat on the grill.

4 to 7 serrano chilies (substitute a milder variety if you prefer), minced

2 to 4 garlic cloves, minced or pressed

1 tablespoon grated fresh ginger

4 tablespoons vegetable oil

¼ cup sake, vodka, or tequila

4 tablespoons soy sauce

4 tablespoons fresh lemon juice

1 to 1½ pounds 1-inch-wide strips of pork or chicken

Combine all the ingredients except the meat and whisk well to blend completely. Add the meat and marinate in the refrigerator 6 hours or more. Remove from the refrigerator half an hour before grilling. Remove the strips from the marinade and reduce the marinade slightly over high heat. Thread the strips on small bamboo skewers and grill about 4 minutes per side on a very hot to hot fire. Serve with the reduced marinade. Serves 2.

BEEF SPICY KEBABS

■■■■■■■■■■■■■■■■■■■■■■■■■

Flank steak seems to be the best cut for this recipe.

¼ cup soy sauce

4 tablespoons vegetable oil

½ cup dry sherry

2 to 4 garlic cloves, minced
  or pressed

4 tablespoons peanut butter

1 to 2 teaspoons dried red
  pepper flakes

1 to 1½ pounds 1-inch-wide
  strips of beef

Combine all the ingredients except the meat and whisk to blend
completely. Marinate, grill, and serve as in the preceding recipe.
Serves 2.

GRILLED SAUSAGES, PEPPERS,
AND POLENTA

■■■■■■■■■■■■■■■■■■■■■■■■

This dish is a real test of your grill surface. The sausages and peppers present no particular challenge; but squares of polenta are
likely to stick to a less-than-perfect grill. Still, if you are feeling
confident in your grilling ability and your grill is scrupulously
clean, well oiled, and preheated, give it a try. If you are feeling
timid, plain boiled polenta cooked on the stove while the sausages are grilling is still a delicious side dish.

3½ cups water

1½ teaspoons salt

1 cup polenta

1½ to 2 pounds sweet or hot
  Italian sausages

3 to 4 red, golden, or green
  bell peppers, sweet Italian
  peppers, or an assortment

Olive oil

Salt and pepper

Dried oregano

One day ahead ■ Bring the water to a boil in a heavy saucepan. Add the salt. Very slowly add the polenta, stirring constantly (you should almost be able to count the grains as they fall into the pot). As the polenta begins to cook and thicken, reduce the heat and simmer, still stirring, until it forms a thick mass and you can see the bottom of the pot as you stir, about 10 minutes. Remove the pan from the heat and pour the polenta into an oiled loaf pan. Refrigerate overnight.

Remove the sausages and polenta from the refrigerator at least 30 minutes before cooking. Unmold the polenta from the loaf pan and slice crosswise into 1-inch-thick slices. Prepare a moderate fire. While all the charcoal is at the flaming stage, put on the peppers. Cook the peppers until the waxy skin is blackened on all sides. Transfer the peppers to a large jar or a paper bag, seal tightly, and let them "sweat" about 15 minutes or until soft.

When the fire has settled down to a glowing stage, grill the sausages. Uncooked sausages an inch or so thick will take 12 to 15 minutes over a moderate fire. Try to leave them alone for at least 5 minutes on the first side to get nice grill marks, then turn the sausages, moving them around the grill as necessary so they cook without scorching.

While the sausages are cooking, peel the blackened skin off the peppers, remove the stems, cores, and seeds, and cut the peppers into strips. Toss the peppers with a little olive oil and season to taste with salt, pepper, and oregano. When the sausages are about 5 minutes away from being done, oil the slices of polenta and add them to the hottest part of the grill. Cook until heated through and slightly crisp, about 7 or 8 minutes. Don't worry if the sausages are done before the polenta, as they will hold their heat for several minutes.

Serve the sausages with strips of pepper and squares of polenta. Drizzle the polenta with a little more olive oil if you like. Serves 4.

Sausages, polenta, and peppers ... bellissimo!

GRILLED LIVER, ONIONS, AND BACON

■ ■ ■ ■ ■ ■ ■ ■ ■ ■ ■ ■ ■ ■ ■ ■ ■ ■ ■ ■

This classic combination works quite well on a charcoal grill. Two servings can easily be cooked on a single-burner hibachi, or four on the double version.

½ bottle beer or ale

1 tablespoon Dijon mustard

½ teaspoon ground black pepper

4 slices (½ inch thick) veal or baby beef liver (about 1 pound)

8 thick bacon slices

1 large onion, quartered or thickly sliced

Combine the beer, mustard, and pepper in a shallow bowl. Add the liver and marinate 30 minutes or so, while the fire is getting started.

Blanch the bacon for a minute or so in a pan of boiling unsalted water, remove, and drain well (this step is optional, but it removes some of the excess salt from the bacon and makes it cook faster on the grill).

Build a hot fire. When the fire is at the flaming stage, cook the onion pieces until tender—slices will only take a few minutes, while quarters will take considerably longer. Remove the onions to a warm plate.

As the fire begins to settle down to the moderate stage, grill the bacon about 2 minutes on a side, or just until it is cooked through but not crisp. Remove the bacon to a warm platter. Drain the liver slices thoroughly and grill them over the hottest part of the fire to the desired degree of doneness—roughly 1½ minutes per side for rare, 2 minutes for medium rare, a little longer for medium. Serve immediately, garnished with the bacon and onions. Polenta, either simply boiled or grilled (see Grilled Sausages, Peppers, and Polenta, preceding), makes a good accompaniment. Serves 4.

Poultry

Commercially available poultry includes the familiar chicken, turkey, duck, and squab, as well as several domesticated "game" birds, including quail, partridge, pheasant, and mallard duck. With care and attention to the flavors and cooking characteristics of each variety, all of these can be charcoal grilled with excellent results.

Marinades and sauces for poultry should be dictated by the choice of bird. Chicken, with its mild flesh and moderate fat content, can go with almost any conceivable sauce or marinade, and it is the easiest bird to grill. Birds with more or less fat content require more specialized cooking techniques; those with more pronounced flavors are better with certain marinades and sauces than others.

The ground rules for grilling all kinds of birds are the same: cook them enough to cook the meat to the bone, but not so much that the meat dries out. With the few exceptions discussed below, poultry should be cooked to the equivalent of "medium" — that is, when the meat near the bones has just become opaque and loses any translucent pinkness—an internal temperature between 175° and 185°F. At this point, juices from near the joints run yellow with just a trace of pink when pierced with a fork or a skewer. The meat begins to dry out if cooked longer.

One of the best ways to preserve the moisture of poultry is to cook it still attached to the bone. The bones absorb heat more slowly than the meat, only to release it into the meat as the cooking proceeds. For this reason, grilling a split chicken mostly with the bone side toward the fire will give better results than cooking mostly on the skin side.

CUTTING TECHNIQUES

Flattening

The easiest way to cook a whole bird on a grill is to split it and flatten it. The following directions, illustrated with a Rock Cornish hen, are suitable for any small bird, from quail to broiling chicken to duck.

1. Remove the giblets from the cavity and place the bird on a cutting board, breast side up. With a heavy chef's knife, cut through the ribs on one side, as close to the backbone as possible.

2. Repeat the process on the other side of the backbone and remove the backbone completely. Save it for stock, along with the neck, giblets, and head and feet, if any. (Optional: skip step 2, and leave the backbone attached on one side of the bird. Also, steps 1 and 2 can be done with poultry shears.)

3. Turn the bird breast side down. Spread the rib cage apart. Make a notch in the end of the breastbone near the wishbone to facilitate splitting and spreading.

4. Turn the bird over again. Flatten it with the heel of your hand.

5. Make 2 slits in the skin near the edge of the breast. Push the ends of the legs through the slits, and tuck the wing tips under the wings. The bird is now ready for marinating and grilling.

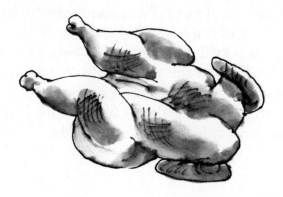

Flattening a bird offers several advantages. It reduces the bird to a manageable, more uniform thickness, reducing the overall cooking time. By exposing all the bones on one side, it allows you to cook the bird mostly from the bone side, reducing the risk of overcooking the meat or charring the skin. Also, the legs help protect the breast meat from the fire, reducing the risk of overcooking the delicate breast meat. And lastly, a flattened bird is easily handled with tongs, a spatula, or a fork, allowing you to move it around the grill as needed to adjust the rate of cooking.

Cutting Up

Cutting a whole bird into serving pieces offers its own advantages. Legs generally take longer to cook than breasts, so they can be started earlier or cooked on a cooler part of the fire. A typical way of cutting up a chicken is to separate the legs and wings from the body, separate the breast from the back through the rib cage, and split the breast into halves attached to the ribs. However, this exposes a lot of breast meat, which can dry out quickly on the grill. A better technique is to leave the breast whole, cracking the breastbone slightly and flattening the whole breast the same way as you flatten a whole bird. This keeps all the meat attached to the bone and encased in skin, so it will be moister after cooking. You can always divide up the breast after cooking.

Splitting and Quartering

Another common method of cutting up poultry is to split the bird in half entirely and cook each half in one piece. This is almost guaranteed to produce overcooked breast meat by the time the leg meat is done, especially on the half that gets cheated out of the breastbone. Cutting each half into a fore- and hindquarter will allow you to put them on the grill at separate times, but you will still have to keep a watchful eye on all that exposed breast meat.

Boning

There are a few cases where boneless pieces of poultry work well on the grill. Whole or half breasts, skinned and boned, cook quickly, making them useful when you have a lot of people to feed and want to use the grill in several shifts over a short period of time. Paillards—half breasts pounded to a thickness of ⅛ inch or so—will cook in even less time. But without the protection of skin and bone, they can dry out with the slightest overcooking, so careful timing is essential.

Making Paillards

1. Split a whole boned breast in half. Run a finger between the two muscles of each half. Cut through the membrane that attaches the smaller muscle on the breastbone side, but leave it attached on the rib side. Fold the smaller muscle back to form a lopsided heart shape.

2. Sprinkle the butterflied breast with a little oil and place it on a sheet of oiled waxed paper or a clean plastic bag. Top with another sheet of oiled paper or plastic. Pound the breast with a meat pounder, a mallet, or the side of a heavy cleaver to a thickness of ⅛ inch. The piece will nearly double in size.

Simple, quick, and elegant: grilled chicken paillards served with a flavorful sauce.

Brochettes

Boneless leg meat of large chickens or turkeys can be cut into cubes, marinated, and grilled *en brochette*. Brochettes of breast meat will dry out quickly, but they can be grilled with extra care.

CHICKEN

Chicken is a favorite in just about every cuisine on earth. One major reason is its versatility. It's hard to imagine any seasoning that can be used for other meats that does not work well with chicken. And while it can be cooked by any method, some of the most memorable chicken dishes are cooked over a charcoal or wood fire.

Chickens suitable for grilling range in size from tiny *poussins* (specially raised baby chickens) of under a pound, to broilers (up to 2½ pounds) and fryers (2 to 3½ pounds). The names are somewhat arbitrary; even larger fryers are young and tender enough for grilling. Fryers are also usually the cheapest whole chickens in any poultry case.

One special form of chicken that is not always thought of as such is Rock Cornish hens (there is no reason to call them game hens: they are no more a game bird than any other chicken). These little birds are a cross of two small breeds of chicken, the Plymouth Rock and the Cornish. They come to market in uniform sizes of around 1¼ pounds, almost always frozen.

The problem with any young (and therefore tender) chicken is one of flavor. Depending on the age and feed of the bird, its freshness, and the taste of the diner, most commercial chicken is quite mild in flavor—often to the point of blandness. Try to find a dealer who specializes in poultry, or an ethnic market that caters to a clientele that demands tasty chickens, and be sure to buy them as fresh as possible. Free-ranging chickens (like the bird Grandma chased around the barnyard) are becoming more widely available as an alternative to the mass-produced variety. They are more expensive, but to those who rate flavor over economy they are worth the price.

Even if you go to great lengths to buy tasty chickens, you still may want to add flavor in the form of a marinade. Long marinating in a wine and herb marinade such as the one on page 116 can create a taste somewhat like that of a wilder bird. On the other hand, the mild flavor of chicken is just right as a foil to highly flavored marinades and sauces.

DEVILED CHICKEN

■■■■■■■■■■■■■■■■■■■■■■■■■■

This recipe can be made with either flattened chicken or chicken parts. There are many versions of this dish. The Italian *pollo al diavolo* uses just lemon juice, olive oil, and plenty of black pepper. The French *poulet à la diable* uses mustard and cayenne. However you make it, it should be "hot as the devil." Making it with liquid hot pepper sauce gives you a more or less instant reading on the hotness of the marinade, while a ground-pepper marinade gets stronger as it sits.

½ cup olive oil

Juice of 1 lemon

2 tablespoons Dijon mustard

3 or 4 dashes Tabasco sauce

1 whole flattened chicken, or 3 to 4 pounds chicken parts

Combine all the ingredients except the chicken in a large bowl. Let the mixture sit a few minutes to allow the flavors to combine. Taste and correct the seasoning. Rub the mixture over the chicken about 30 minutes before grilling.

Build a moderate fire in a covered or open grill. When the fire settles down to the glowing stage, start the chicken on the skin side. Turn after about 10 minutes and continue cooking from the bone side until the juices run yellow when the chicken is pierced with a fork or a skewer near the joints, about 25 to 35 minutes total cooking time. Baste frequently with the excess marinade while grilling. Serves 4.

Olive oil is the favored oil of most grill chefs.

SPICY INDONESIAN CHICKEN

■ ■

Prepare Spicy Indonesian Marinade, page 69. Marinate 3 pounds cut-up chicken (or turkey) or 2 pounds chicken (or turkey) brochettes in the marinade for several hours or overnight in the refrigerator; remove from the refrigerator a half hour before grilling. Grill as for Deviled Chicken, preceding. Serves 4.

TANDOORI CHICKEN

■ ■

Remove the skin from a fryer or 3 to 4 pounds of chicken parts. Slash the meat at intervals to allow the marinade to penetrate. Rub Tandoori Marinade with Saffron, page 67, over the meat, rubbing it well into all the cuts. Marinate the chicken for several hours or, preferably, overnight in the refrigerator; remove from the refrigerator about a half hour before grilling. A whole chicken can be spit-roasted or flattened and grilled over a moderate fire; chicken parts can be cooked directly on the grill or in a folding wire grill. A flattened chicken will take about 30 minutes on the grill, a spit-roasted bird 45 minutes to an hour; juices will run clear when the chicken is pierced near the joints with a fork or skewer. Baste occasionally with 2 tablespoons melted butter combined with the remaining marinade. Serves 4.

a skewered chicken...

ready to roast.

MOCK GAME BIRDS

■■■■■■■■■■■■■■■■■■■■■■■■■■

A spicy port wine marinade will give any meat a more gamelike flavor: pork will taste more like wild boar, lamb more like venison, and Rock Cornish "game" hens will actually taste a little like game birds. The marinade recipe makes about 3 cups, sufficient for 4 Rock Cornish hens, 2 fryers, a pork or lamb shoulder, or 4 to 5 pounds pork or lamb chops.

2 cups ruby port

½ cup red wine vinegar

¼ cup olive oil

1 teaspoon coriander seeds

1 teaspoon fennel seeds

2 teaspoons juniper berries

1 teaspoon cracked black
   peppercorns

1 small onion or 2 scallions,
   roughly chopped

3 garlic cloves, lightly crushed

1 tablespoon minced fresh
   ginger

4 Rock Cornish hens

Combine the port, vinegar, and oil in a large stainless steel or glass bowl. Combine the coriander, fennel, juniper berries, and peppercorns in a mortar or spice grinder and grind coarsely. Add the spices to the bowl along with the onion, garlic, and ginger.

Flatten the birds and marinate them overnight or, preferably, 2 or 3 days, in the refrigerator. Turn the birds frequently to distribute the marinade evenly. Remove the birds from the refrigerator half an hour before grilling. Grill over a moderate fire, starting with 8 to 10 minutes on the skin side and finishing the cooking from the bone side, about 20 minutes total cooking time (the juices will run clear when the chicken is pierced near the joints with a fork or skewer). Serves 4.

Note A whole bird per person is a generous serving. Light appetites or large menus may dictate half a bird per person.

DUCK

■▪■▪■▪■▪■▪■▪■▪■▪■▪■▪■▪■▪■▪■▪■▪■▪■▪■▪■

Most duck preparations are complicated by the need to deal with the enormous amount of fat contained in each bird. Usually some form of slow cooking is required to melt away most of the fat. Oven-roasting the bird to the rare stage is the usual preliminary step in restaurants that serve grilled duck. In order to avoid overcooking the breast meat, some cooks roast the whole duck just until the breast is rare, carve the breast away with the wings attached, then continue roasting until the legs are cooked to the same degree of doneness. The separate pieces can then be finished off over a hot grill, crisping the skin and finishing the cooking.

Another approach is to simply roast the whole bird in a kettle-type grill. Before cooking, prick the skin with a fork or skewer all over the surface of the duck, especially at the lower edge of the breast and thighs, and roast over a drip pan. Whole ducks can also be trussed and spit-roasted, again after piercing the skin liberally to allow the melted fat to escape.

Heading south to avoid the grilling season.

CHARCOAL-GRILLED DUCK

■ ■

This recipe, which combines Western seasonings and charcoal grilling with Eastern techniques of dry marinating and steaming, was inspired by Barbara Tropp's "Fragrant Crispy Duck" in *The Modern Art of Chinese Cooking* (New York: William Morrow, 1982). Her recipe uses Chinese seasonings, of course, and finishes with deep-frying the duck, but the preliminary steps of marinating the duck in a seasoned salt mixture and steaming it to render most of the fat are equally applicable to other kinds of duck cookery. Also, while the original Chinese version is steamed until very tender to facilitate eating with chopsticks, the steaming here is much shorter, being just a means of eliminating some of the fat.

Because the duck will still drip a fair amount of fat while on the grill, flames may be a problem, so a covered kettle grill is best for this recipe. However, you can cook it on an open grill without too much flaming if you keep the fire moderate. The duck will be mostly cooked in the process of steaming, so the purpose of grilling is mainly to heat it through and crisp the skin.

1 duck, 4 to 5 pounds	2 teaspoons fresh thyme
1 bay leaf	¼ cup coarse kosher salt
2 teaspoons fresh rosemary	1 teaspoon ground black pepper
1 teaspoon fresh sage leaves	

(Note: If using dried herbs, use
   only half as much)

Remove the head and feet, if any, from the duck (the neck may be left attached, removed and cooked separately, or removed altogether and reserved for making stock). Rinse the bird thoroughly, inside and out, and wipe dry. Split the duck down the back and flatten it, removing the backbone or leaving it attached, as you wish (see page 110). Remove any easily accessible fat.

Chop or crumble the herbs thoroughly and combine them with the salt and pepper. Rub the mixture all over both sides of the bird, place it on a deep plate to catch any juices, and refrigerate for at least 6 hours or, preferably, overnight.

Let the duck come to room temperature before steaming. For a steaming vessel, you will need a wok or other large covered pot at least 14 inches in diameter and deep enough to hold the duck on a plate at least an inch above boiling water. Bring the water in the steamer to a rolling boil while you position the duck, skin side up, on a deep plate placed on a steaming rack or trivet (a large heatproof glass pie plate works very well). If the ends of the duck hang over the edge of the plate, put a piece of aluminum foil under the overhanging part so that the fat will drain onto the plate. Have a bulb baster ready to draw off the fat as it renders out of the bird.

When the water has come to a vigorous boil, place the duck in the steamer on its plate. Cover, bring the water back to a full boil, then reduce the heat slightly to maintain a good head of steam. After 15 minutes of steaming, use the baster to draw off the fat that has accumulated on the plate.

Continue steaming the duck, removing the rendered fat every 10 minutes or so, until the duck has rendered a cup or more of fat, about 45 minutes total cooking time. Remove the plate from the steamer, tip the duck to drain off as much liquid as possible, and let the duck cool on a wire rack set over a cookie sheet to collect any more drippings. The duck can be left to air dry for several hours at room temperature, or overnight in the refrigerator. (Thorough air drying will give a slightly crisper skin, but it is not essential. In fact, if you don't have the time to air dry the duck, it can be grilled right away with excellent results.)

Grill the duck over a moderate fire, starting on the skin side, but doing most of the cooking from the bone side. Turn the bird skin side down again for a last few minutes of cooking to finish crisping the skin. Serves 2 to 4.

SQUAB

▰▰▰▰▰▰▰▰▰▰▰▰▰▰▰▰▰▰▰▰▰▰▰▰▰▰

Of all domestic birds, squab (young pigeon) bears the most resemblance to a wild bird in flavor. The meat has a slight liver flavor, but is without the strong gaminess of some wild birds. It is also much more tender than any wild game, making it ideal for dry-heat cooking. The main drawback of squab is the cost, about $5 a pound at this writing. A 1-pound drawn bird, with head, neck, and feet, makes a single serving, putting it a bit out of everyday range. But the special flavor of squab is worth an occasional splurge.

GRILLED SQUABS

■■■■■■■■■■■■■■■■■■■■■■■

To prepare squabs for grilling, split them down the back and flatten them. Save the backbones, heads, and feet for a delicious stock that can be used as the base for another sauce.

Marinate the birds for several hours or overnight in the port wine and herb marinade for Mock Game Birds (page 116), or better still, in the style of Jeremiah Tower at the Santa Fe Bar & Grill, in a purée of unsweetened fresh or frozen raspberries with a little fresh thyme and vinegar. The sweet and tart flavor of the marinade offers a delicious counterpoint to the rich flavor of the meat. Refrigerate the birds while they are marinating; remove them from the refrigerator half an hour before serving.

To preserve the distinctive flavor and color of squabs, cook them only to the medium-rare stage (about 15 minutes over a hot fire). If you use the berry marinade, be careful not to cook too long on the skin side, or the sugar in the fruit will burn and give a bitter flavor. Serve 1 squab per person.

TURKEY

Roasting a whole turkey, or smoking it prior to roasting in the oven, is one of the most spectacular (and most popular) uses for a kettle grill, and has in fact become the standard Thanksgiving turkey-cooking method for many families. But the turkey industry is doing its best to get us to eat turkey all year round. Fresh turkey parts are becoming increasingly available in supermarkets and offer an interesting and reasonably priced alternative to other poultry. Whole thighs are the most practical cut for cooking directly on a grill; for some reason, drumsticks are harder to cook without overcooking. Turkey breast is very lean and prone to drying, so it is not advised unless you watch it very carefully and practice split-second timing. Leg meat can be cut up for brochettes.

Any marinade or sauce that is suitable for chicken (which includes almost anything) can be used with turkey.

ROAST TURKEY

A charcoal-roasted turkey is hard to beat for a holiday meal. An important side benefit is that there is one less item to prepare in the kitchen, which helps to ease the frenzy associated with cooking an elaborate feast. A covered kettle grill is all but essential to charcoal-roast a large bird. It is not necessary to baste a bird in a covered grill—just make sure the coals are producing adequate heat. We think it's best to roast the bird unstuffed; the stuffing can be made in the oven and moistened with the juices caught in the drip pan. Because it is hard to judge exactly how long it will take a turkey to cook, always allow yourself extra time. A large turkey should rest at least 30 minutes after grilling, while you prepare the other dishes.

1 turkey, 18 to 22 pounds
(make sure it will fit inside
the grill with the cover on)

2 or more onions

2 cups celery tops

4 tablespoons butter

Dried sage

Salt and pepper

Melted butter or vegetable oil

Remove the neck and giblets from the bird; reserve for making gravy, if desired. Wash the bird thoroughly with cold water and pat dry with paper towels to absorb as much moisture, inside and out, as possible. Roughly chop the onions and celery. Cut the butter into small pieces. Toss the onions, celery, butter, sage, salt, and pepper together in a large bowl. Place a handful of the mixture in the neck cavity. Pull the skin over the neck and fasten behind the back with a small metal skewer. Put the rest of the onion and celery mixture (which is for flavoring only) inside the cavity of the bird. Lock the wings behind the back and tie the legs and tail together securely, or retuck the legs under the band of skin. Using the melted butter or vegetable oil, baste the outer surface of the bird completely and add a good sprinkling of salt and freshly ground pepper. Rather than relying on the "pop-up" thermometers that come in some turkeys, it's best to use your own meat thermometer. Insert the thermometer into the center of the thickest part of the thigh, not touching the bone.

Prepare a fire using the indirect method on page 46. Use a drip pan provided by the manufacturer, or any metal pan about the same size as the turkey, to catch the juice. Place the drip pan in the center of the fire grate. The bird should be placed breast side up in the center of the grill, over the drip pan, directly on the grill or on a roast holder. An alternate method, which produces excellent results, is to arrange the coals on opposite sides of the fire grate, put the grill in place, and then place the turkey on a small rack in a roasting pan. There's no problem with burning the bottom of the bird this way, and there will be more juices in the pan. Count on 11 to 13 minutes per pound to reach an internal temperature of 185°F. Check to make sure the coals are still producing heat every hour to an hour and a half. If you are cooking a large turkey you may want to start additional coals in a large can or flower pot to add during the cooking process (see page 51). Adding cold charcoal to a slow fire can further reduce the temperature until the new coals catch, resulting in an uneven temperature pattern. If you've tied the legs together with string, cut it when the bird is about two-thirds done to allow for more even cooking. Serves 12 to 15.

SMOKED TURKEY

■ ■

Smoked turkey can be a particularly distinctive and delicious part of a holiday buffet or groaning board. The procedure, as described on page 51, is a long one, but the results are worth the effort. Prepare the turkey (somewhere in the range of 20 pounds) as in the previous recipe for roast whole turkey, but leave the legs untied, and don't place on a roasting pan on the grill, as described in the alternate method above. Don't worry about a thermometer at this stage; you'll finish roasting the bird over a hotter charcoal fire or in the oven. Prepare your fire and smoking chips according to the instructions given on page 51. A 20-pound turkey will take between 4 and 5 hours to smoke; you'll know it's done when the skin has developed a mahogany-brown hue.

When the smoking process is complete, allow the turkey to cool and, if you are not going to finish the cooking process and eat it that day, wrap it tightly in plastic wrap or foil. At this point it is possible to store it in the refrigerator for 2 to 3 days.

On the day you are going to eat the turkey, remove it from the refrigerator and allow it to come to room temperature. Insert a meat thermometer into the thickest part of the thigh, making sure it does not touch the bone. Baste the bird with vegetable oil or melted butter and roast in a 325°F oven or in a covered kettle grill using the indirect method described in the previous recipe, until the thermometer reaches 185°F. This process usually takes about 2 hours. When the desired temperature has been reached, remove the turkey from the grill or oven, allow to cool for 10 or 15 minutes, and serve it forth.

Note Don't rely on the pop-up timers that come already inserted in some turkeys; there's something about the smoking process that renders the button impotent. A 20-pound turkey will serve 12 to 15 people, with lots of leftovers.

TURKEY BROCHETTES

■ ■

The trend towards eating more fish and poultry has resulted in the appearance of fresh turkey parts at most meat counters. The brochettes in this recipe are cut from half a turkey breast. If your first thought is, "Doesn't the breast meat dry out in a hurry over the grill?" the answer is yes, but it doesn't have to. Follow the directions given below carefully and you'll have moist, delicious turkey meat like you've probably never had before.

⅓ cup olive or other vegetable oil

¼ cup soy sauce

½ cup dry vermouth

Juice of ½ lemon

1½ tablespoons grated fresh ginger

2 to 3 garlic cloves, minced or pressed

About 2 teaspoons ground black pepper

1 fresh turkey breast half, skinned and cut into 1½-to-2-inch cubes

Mix the first 7 ingredients together in a large stainless steel or glass bowl. Whisk to blend well. Add the cubed turkey meat and toss to coat evenly. Cover the bowl and marinate in the refrigerator for 4 to 6 hours. Remove the brochettes from the refrigerator half an hour before serving.

Thread the turkey brochettes on large metal skewers. Pack them rather tightly together, as this helps to keep the meat from drying out. Grill over a moderate charcoal fire for a total of approximately 15 minutes, turning 3 or 4 times.

Put 1 skewer on each plate and serve with a dipping sauce (page 78–83) or various chutneys. Serve with cold beer. Serves 4.

Fish

Charcoal grilling is one of the most versatile and one of the best methods of fish cookery. Yet many backyard grillers, perfectly at home cooking anything from hamburgers to spareribs to lamb chops on the grill, rarely try any fish other than swordfish or salmon steaks. Unfortunately, they are missing out on some of the most delicious dishes ever to come off a charcoal grill.

Just about any type of fish can be successfully grilled with practice and attention to preparation and cooking time. While grilling fish is a simple technique, it is not a particularly easy one to completely master. No other type of food is so unforgiving of overcooking, and the difference between a perfectly cooked piece of fish and a dry one is often a matter of seconds, or a minute or two at the most.

BASIC CUTS FOR GRILLING

The way a piece of fish is cut up or otherwise prepared for the grill is essential to the cooking process. Just as certain cuts of meat are ideal for thin paillards but disastrous as thick steaks, so some species of fish have radically different cooking characteristics according to how they are cut. It's important to choose the appropriate shape for each fish, based on its fat content, moisture content, and density. Here are some of the options:

Round This refers to the whole fish just as it comes out of the water. Some very small fish, such as smelt or anchovies, are cooked and eaten whole. Skewering several fish together or using a hinged grill is helpful, as individual small fish might fall through the regular grill.

Dressed This refers to a whole fish, gutted, scaled, and with the gills removed, but the head left on. Theoretically any fish that will fit on the grill can be cooked in this form, but in practice, it is best for fish of a pound or less. *Pan-dressed* fish are the same as dressed, but with the head removed. Either form is ideal for small, delicate fish such as trout or sole. Cooking the fish on the bones preserves its moisture, while the skin cooks to a delicious crispness.

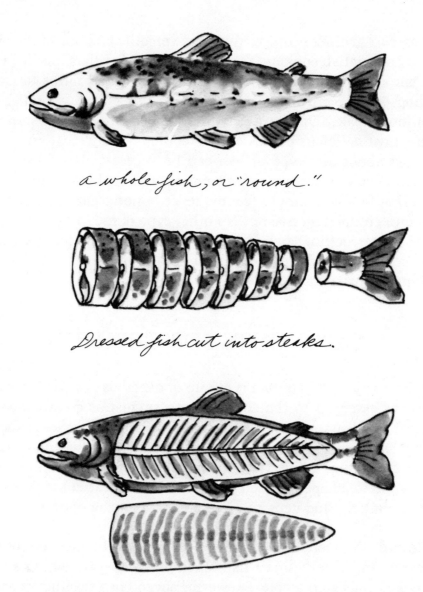

a whole fish, or "round."

Dressed fish cut into steaks.

a fillet cut from one side of the fish.

Steaks Steaks are sections of fish cut crosswise into pieces about an inch thick. This is the most familiar form for swordfish, shark, halibut, and salmon in most markets. The thickness of steaks determines the cooking time, of course, but also the ideal amount of heat. The rule goes like this: higher heat for thinner steaks, so the outside will sear quickly before the inside becomes overcooked; lower heat for thicker steaks, so the inside can cook before the outside becomes charred.

Fillets Fillets are probably the most versatile form of fish for grilling. Any fish over a pound is typically filleted first, then cut up, if necessary, into smaller pieces for serving. These may be *slices*, basically 1-inch steaks cut on a diagonal, or *scallops*, similarly cut pieces cut thinner. Firm fish fillets can also be cut up into *cubes* of an inch or so, to be cooked on skewers. Whole fillets or odd pieces can also be wrapped in edible leaves and grilled in their wrapping (see the trout recipe, page 136).

Let's take a closer look at the different ways of cutting up a fish and see how they affect the cooking process. A 9-pound dressed salmon, for example, will yield 2 whole fillets of about 3 pounds each. At the tail end, the fillet is less than ½ inch thick, while near the head it is well over an inch. You could cut the fillet straight across into sections of equal weight, but some would be as thick as they are wide and would take quite a bit longer to cook than others. However, cutting the fillet on a diagonal into slices of the same weight produces more uniformity in thickness. Slices from near the head are no thicker than the tail section, so they will all cook at about the same rate. Each portion also looks larger because it covers more of the plate.

Cutting a large fillet into slices exposes more of the surface area of the fish, which can work either for or against you. On the positive side, there is more surface to absorb flavors from the marinade and the charcoal smoke. However, the increased surface area also means that the slice of fish will dry out more quickly in cooking, making timing more critical. If you are a little unsure of your skill in grilling fish, choose somewhat thicker pieces and moderate heat.

SOME POINTERS ON COOKING FISH

Whatever cut of fish you are grilling, there are several points to keep in mind to avoid the most common faults: overcooking, undercooking, and fish sticking to the grill.

1. Use a hot enough fire. More problems come from too little heat than too much. If the fire is too cold, it will not sear the surface of the fish, so much of the moisture will be lost before the fish is cooked.

2. Arrange the fire with hotter and cooler spots by concentrating or spreading out the coals. This gives you the flexibility to move each piece around according to how it is cooking.

3. Preheat the grill and keep the grill surface clean and well oiled. Fish is more likely to stick to a cold grill, or to one that is encrusted with burnt barbecue sauce.

4. Remember that the fish will continue to cook slightly after it is removed from the grill. Learn to judge when each piece is almost done and then take it off the grill at that exact point.

5. An easy way to test doneness of a piece of fish is with a small bamboo or metal skewer. Probe into the thickest part of the fish with the tip of the skewer and feel the resistance of the flesh. Practicing with a piece of uncooked fish will help you get the feel: raw fish offers more resistance because you are actually cutting through the connective tissue between the muscle fibers. As the fish cooks, the protein that makes up this tissue relaxes to the point that the skewer will slip in with little resistance. Cooked beyond this point, however, the fish loses its moisture rapidly. When the fish "flakes easily with a fork," the traditional test of doneness, it is already too dry and overdone.

6. Pay attention to how you place the fish on the grill and how you handle it. Orienting the fish perpendicular to the grill bars minimizes the contact of the fish with the grill, reducing the chance of sticking. Avoid moving the fish too often, as each move gives it one more chance to stick to the grill. Most fish should be turned only once, and served with the first-cooked side face up.

WHICH FISH FOR THE GRILL?

The following is a guide to popular fish types for grilling. They are grouped into categories according to their cooking characteristics—fat content, moisture content, density, and flavor—and each category is headed by a single fish that can serve as an archetype. Once you have mastered cooking sea bass, for example, you can apply the same techniques, marinades, and sauces to striped bass, redfish, corbina, drum, or speckled trout. The list is arranged from richer fish to leaner types. Richer fish, such as salmon or tuna, are slightly less prone to drying out on the grill, so they are a good place for novice fish grillers to begin. For specific fish recipes, see pages 135–141.

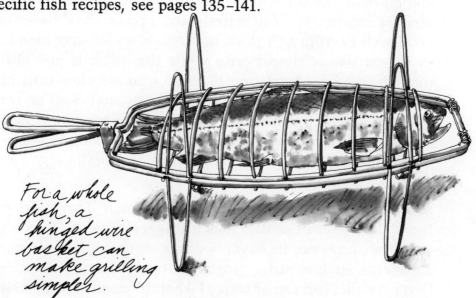

For a whole fish, a hinged wire basket can make grilling simpler.

Salmon *also steelhead and large trout* This is easily the most popular fish for outdoor cooking in the West, and one of the most popular throughout the country. With its rich flesh and distinctive flavor, salmon really needs no marinade, except perhaps a little oil and a mild herb such as dill or thyme (though salmon basted with teriyaki sauce is quite popular). Simply grilled salmon should be served with a mild-flavored sauce, such as *beurre blanc* (page 85). Best cuts: steaks, fillets, slices, scallops, brochettes.

Trout *also coho or "baby salmon"* Most of the trout available in our markets is raised on farms in Idaho or other western states. These farms produce uniformly sized, fairly inexpensive fish with relatively little flavor, especially when compared to wild trout. Coho (silver) salmon are now being farmed in the Northwest, and come to the market anywhere from 8 to 12 ounces in weight. These, too, have only a trace of the flavor of the wild version. Both can benefit from a marinade with a strong herb such as rosemary or fennel. Adding herb branches to the fire is especially helpful here. Best cuts: dressed, pan-dressed.

Tuna *also bonito, yellowtail, mahi-mahi, marlin, barracuda, and bluefish* Not all of these fish are related, but they share a high fat content, fairly firm flesh, and a pronounced flavor that takes well to grilling. A thick tuna steak, grilled over high heat so the outside is almost crisp while the inside is just heated through, can be a revelation to those who associate tuna only with sandwiches. Soy-based basting sauces work well on tuna, as do oil and herb marinades; a colorful compound butter (see page 76) melting on top is the ideal sauce. Best cuts: pan-dressed (for smaller types), steaks, fillets, slices, brochettes.

Mackerel *also jack mackerel and jacksmelt* This most maligned of fishes can be delicious if it is really fresh. Even when very fresh, however, its flavor is strong, so use equally strong ingrendients, such as garlic, ginger, or strong herbs to balance the flavor. Smaller fish can be cooked whole (dressed or pan-dressed) or larger ones can be filleted. Best cuts: dressed, pan-dressed, fillets.

Eel Eel really fits into no other category. Its flesh is rich and tasty, but somewhat bony. Skinning an eel is a tricky business, but necessary. And they tend to be expensive. Still, if you can find them (and a fish dealer who will skin them for you), try them cut into 1- to 2-inch lengths and marinated in teriyaki-style sauce. They are delicious! Best cuts: steaks, chunks.

Sablefish *also known as black cod or butterfish* This is another fish in a category by itself. It is very popular in the Pacific Northwest where most of it is caught, but less so in other parts of the country to which it is shipped. The reason may be that in most markets outside the Northwest it is nearly always sold in fillet form. Grilling fillets of "butterfish," as it is widely known, is an exercise in frustration: the soft flesh begins to fall apart as it cooks, making it just about impossible to get off the grill in one piece. If you can find it in steak form, however (or buy a whole fish and cut it into steaks yourself), the skin and bone of each steak help to hold it together. The flavor is mild but agreeable, and takes well to most marinades. Best cut: steaks.

Smelt *also sardine, anchovy, and herring* These small, oily fish take well to grilling, especially since they are best when thoroughly cooked. Best cuts: round, pan-dressed, fillets (skin on), rolled fillets *en brochette.* A convenient way to prepare them for grilling is the "butterfly double fillet" method, as follows:

1. Pull off the head, along with any entrails that come with it.

2. Cut open the belly of the fish with a small knife and pull away the remaining entrails. Don't worry about cleaning it thoroughly; the entrails will be removed with the bones in the following steps.

3. Place the fish belly side down on the cutting board and press it down until one fillet separates from the bones.

4. Turn the fish over and peel away the backbone of the other fillet. All the ribs should come away with the backbone, leaving the two fillets attached to each other by the back skin. Rinse the fillets and pat dry, marinate briefly in oil and mild herbs, and grill the fish flat or rolled and secured with a skewer.

(continued)

Sturgeon This primitive fish is best known for its roe (caviar), but the flesh makes good eating, too. While it is frequently cut into steaks, you might prefer the flavor of a skinned fillet, as the skin can sometimes harbor a slightly muddy flavor. Because the meat is very dense, it should be sliced into thin scallops, no more than ½ inch thick, for easy grilling. Two or 3 scallops may be necessary per serving if the fillet is small. Either mild or strong herbs can be used for the marinade and the sauce. Best cuts: steaks, scallops.

White sea bass *also striped bass, corbina, redfish, drum, and speckled trout* These moderately rich and very tasty fish have especially firm flesh, making them ideal for grilling in fillet form. Large fillets can be cut into slices or scallops or 1-inch cubes for brochettes. Just about any marinade or sauce will work with these versatile fish. Best cuts: fillets, slices, scallops, brochettes.

Red snapper *also black sea bass and grouper* This category is a bit leaner, milder, and sweeter tasting than the previous one, but their cooking characteristics are otherwise the same as those of the white sea bass group. Note that we are talking about the "real" red snapper *(Lutjanus campechanus)* from the Gulf of Mexico and southern Atlantic coast, not the many Pacific rockfish varieties *(Sebastes spp.)* sold as "snapper" or even "red snapper." Best cuts: fillets, slices, scallops, brochettes.

Swordfish If salmon is the favorite in the West, swordfish is the undisputed champion fish for grilling in the East. Steaks anywhere from ½ inch to 1 inch thick are perfect for grilling, but they generally need an oil marinade and sometimes frequent basting to keep them from drying out. The almost beefy flavor of swordfish goes well with compound butters, béarnaise sauce, and other typical accompaniments to grilled beef steaks. Best cuts: steaks, brochettes.

Shark Just a few years ago, fishermen could not give away shark meat, and everyone heard stories of unscrupulous dealers and restaurateurs trying to pass off shark steaks as swordfish or, cut into circles, as scallops. Now shark is quite popular. Larger fish are cut into steaks, while smaller types, such as leopard shark and dogfish, are filleted and cut into slices. Most shark should be soaked in a mild acid solution for about 30 minutes (lemon juice or vinegar in water, or even milk) to neutralize any ammonia flavor that might develop as a result of the shark's metabolism. After soaking, the steaks can be treated like swordfish. Shark with Recado Rojo, page 140, is an interesting Mexican treatment. Best cuts: steaks, slices, scallops, brochettes.

Halibut *also turbot* These large flat fish are widely available in frozen, bandsaw-cut steaks. Unfortunately, the freezing and thawing process robs them of much of their moisture. Even with marinades and diligent basting, a grilled frozen halibut steak is likely to be dry. However, if you can ever come by fresh halibut, including the smaller California species, by all means try grilling it in fillet form. Its flesh is firm, sweet, moist, and altogether delicious. Use a mild oil and herb marinade that lets its delicate flavor come through, and a similarly understated sauce such as an herb-flavored *beurre blanc* (page 85). Best cuts: steaks, slices, scallops.

Rockfish *also cod, lingcod, haddock, tilefish, cabezon, ocean perch, and others* This is a broad category of mild, lean white-fleshed fish that can be lumped together for our purposes (rockfish, by the way, is the more correct name for the dozens of species of the genus *Sebastes* caught on the Pacific Coast and generally sold as "rock cod," "Pacific snapper," "ocean perch," and even "red snapper"). All of these fish are usually filleted, and they are easy to grill in whole fillets or cut up into sections. Their mild flavor goes well with all types of marinades and sauces, so they can fit into just about any menu. Best cuts: pan-dressed, fillets, slices, brochettes.

Sole *also flounder, sand dab, and John Dory* While these small flat fish vary quite a bit in flavor and texture, they are similar enough to treat as a group here. Small soles and sand dabs are excellent pan dressed and grilled over charcoal without any marinade; in fact, many regular customers at San Francisco's old Dalmatian fish grills rarely order anything else. The skin cooks to a delightful crispness, while the meat stays moist and tender because of the heat-moderating effect of the bones. Two or three fish typically make a serving. A 1- to 1½-pound petrale sole or small flounder can be grilled the same way, with similar results. Curiously, oiling the skin of flat fish makes them more likely to stick to the grill. Larger fish are generally filleted, though fillets of flat fish are notoriously difficult to grill without overcooking. Best cuts: dressed, pan-dressed, fillets.

Monkfish *also known as angler* This is another fish that until recently had almost no market in this country, despite the fact that it has been prized in Europe for centuries. It has very firm, sweet flesh with a slight shellfish flavor. Monkfish is one of the most delicious fish to grill, but it requires some special handling. The tail (the only portion to come to market) is covered with a loose, thick skin, which is fairly easy to remove, and underneath that is a thin but tough transparent membrane that must be removed before cooking, otherwise it shrinks rapidly in cooking and distorts the shape of the fillets. Large fillets (over 1 inch thick) should be butterflied to reduce them to a thickness of ¾ inch or less, or else cut into crosswise slices to grill *en brochette*. Either way, grilled monkfish is quite juicy and tasty, with a texture not unlike lobster. Mild herb marinades are best suited to its flavor. Best cuts: fillets, brochettes.

GRILLED WHOLE SALMON

■ ■

Every year, sometime in late October, a small group of old friends and kindred spirits gathers together at a historic apple ranch high in the western hills above the Napa Valley. It is a ritualistic event celebrating the harvest, the change of the seasons, and the approach of the holiday season.

Although this event begins with fresh oysters and clams, it revolves around a whole grilled salmon, accompanied with a tossed green salad, *rösti* potatoes (page 162), and a *buerre blanc.*

Grilling a whole salmon is not for the faint of heart, and to do it properly, you have to have your wits intact. It's also not the best solitary activity—it definitely helps to have people around for kibbitzing and moral support. Whatever you do, don't wrap the salmon in foil; with that decision, you're better off poaching or baking the fish indoors.

1 medium (5 or 6 pounds) whole fresh salmon, dressed (head and tail intact)

1½ to 2 lemons, thinly sliced

1 large onion, thinly sliced

3 or 4 celery tops, with leaves

Fresh dill, if available (if not, a healthy sprinkling of dried)

Vegetable oil

Beurre Blanc, page 85, made with equal parts lemon juice and vinegar and a sprinkling of capers

Lemon wedges

Watercress

Wash the fish thoroughly with cold water and pat dry to remove as much excess moisture as possible. Layer the lemon and onion slices, celery tops, and dill evenly in the cavity of the fish. Sew the cavity shut with a large needle and white cotton string, using the most rudimentary of stitches. Using your hand or a basting brush, oil the fish lightly from head to tail.

Place the fish on a clean grill over a hot-to-moderate fire in a covered grill. If you don't have a covered grill, use a lid from a turkey roaster, or fashion a foil tent to cover the fish. Believe me, you do not want to test your luck by turning the fish more than once, so count on about 12 minutes per side. When it comes time to flip the fish on its other side, whisper a quick prayer, and put 2 spatulas of equal size under the fish, each a third of the way from the ends of the fish. There is no graceful way to do this, so just do it as best you can, using a lot of body English. Don't worry if, in flipping the fish, you've rolled it too far to one side of the grill; simply push it discreetly, using the spatulas, back to where it belongs.

After the requisite time on the grill, when the fish tests done by the skewer test (page 128), remove it carefully to a large platter, garnish it with lemon wedges and watercress, and present it to the clamouring horde. Cut and serve as you would a whole poached salmon—that is, work on one side at a time, cutting slices only halfway through (just to the rib cage), and lift off the meat using a narrow spatula, starting from the backbone of the fish, easing down to the belly. Pass the beurre blanc and enjoy! Serves 10 to 12.

TROUT GRILLED IN GRAPE LEAVES

■ ■

For each serving, place a sprig of fresh thyme in the cavity of a dressed 8-ounce rainbow trout. Flatten out a large (at least 5 inches across) canned grape leaf, dull side up. Place the fish across the leaf near the stem end, tuck the stem inside the cavity of the fish, and roll the leaf tightly around the fish. Brush the wrapped fish with olive oil. Grill over a hot fire until done by the skewer test, about 7 minutes. Throw some sprigs of fresh thyme on the fire as the trout cooks. Serve with lemon wedges.

The same approach works with any small freshwater fish such as perch or bluegill, or with small mackerel or its relatives. Larger fish may require more than one leaf.

STURGEON WITH LIME BEURRE BLANC

■ ■

Lime *beurre blanc* is an unusual variation of the standard beurre blanc recipe found on page 85. Because the flavor of lime is quite pronounced, this sauce is particularly well suited for meaty fish such as sturgeon, sea bass, or swordfish.

1½ tablespoons chopped shallots

¼ cup white wine vinegar

¼ cup fresh lime juice

¼ cup heavy cream

1 cup (2 sticks) unsalted butter, cut into a total of 16 pieces

½ teaspoon grated lime zest (optional)

Freshly ground white pepper

1½ to 2 pounds sturgeon fillet, in slices or scallops (page 127)

4 thin lime slices, for garnish

Add the chopped shallots, vinegar, and lime juice to a medium-sized saucepan. Bring to a boil and reduce heat slightly. Reduce the contents to approximately 3 tablespoons liquid. Add the cream, bring the mixture back to a boil, and quickly whisk in 2 or 3 pieces of butter at a time, adding more just as the last pieces are almost dissolved. The sauce will be thick and foamy. Add the lime zest if you prefer a stronger lime flavor. Add ground white pepper to taste. Keep the sauce warm over low heat, or pour it into a Thermos until needed. Grill the fish fillets over a moderate fire until done, using the skewer test on page 128. Pour approximately ¼ cup sauce over each fillet and garnish with a wedge of lime. Serves 4, with a little extra sauce.

Courtesy of Norman's restaurant, Berkeley, California.

MARLIN WITH
SPICY CILANTRO BUTTER

■ ■

This recipe from Norman's restaurant in Berkeley uses fresh marlin fillets. If you can't find them, try fresh tuna, or one of the other fish listed under *tuna* on page 130.

1 cup (2 sticks) unsalted butter, at room temperature, cut into pieces

2 tablespoons minced cilantro

1 teaspoon minced jalapeño or serrano chili

2 teaspoons minced garlic

1 teaspoon minced fresh ginger

4 marlin fillets, approximately 8 ounces each

Put the butter into a mixing bowl and beat (using an electric beater or fork) until fluffy. Add the cilantro, chili, garlic, and ginger and mix well. The mixture can then be dropped by the tablespoonful onto a piece of waxed paper and refrigerated until needed. Grill the fish over a moderate fire until done, using the skewer test on page 128. Place a dollop of the flavored butter on top of each hot fish fillet. If desired, you can also gently heat this mixture and use it as a hot butter sauce (see page 83).

Cilantro may be an acquired taste, but once acquired it may become a habit.

SWORDFISH
WITH SAUCE NIÇOISE

■ ■

This is a full-flavored sauce to complement a full-flavored fish. If swordfish is not available, use sturgeon, fresh tuna, shark, or marlin.

6 tablespoons butter

Juice of 1 lemon

1 or 2 garlic cloves, minced or pressed

2 anchovies, mashed with a fork*

1 tablespoon minced parsley

Freshly ground pepper

4 swordfish steaks

Chopped parsley

Lemon wedges

Melt the butter in a small saucepan. Add the lemon, garlic, mashed anchovies, parsley, and pepper to taste. Cook over low heat, stirring occasionally, for 10 minutes. Keep over very low heat until ready to use. Grill the swordfish steaks over a hot fire until done by the skewer test (see page 128). Pour the *niçoise* sauce evenly over the 4 steaks. Garnish with a sprinkling of parsley and a wedge of lemon. Serves 4.

*Substitute 1 tablespoon Pâté d'Olive (available at specialty markets) for anchovies if there is an anchovy-hater in your crowd.

The flavors of Nice... redolent with garlic.

SHARK
WITH RECADO ROJO

■ ■

Around the Yucatán Peninsula, a favorite way of cooking fish is
to season it with a paste of ground *achiote* (*annatto* seed), other
spices, and citrus juice, and grill it over a charcoal fire. The traditional fish is a small shark or dogfish, which is butterfly filleted
and left attached to the skin, seasoned with the *recado rojo* and
cooked in a folding wire grill. When the fish is done, it is served
in small pieces inside warm tortillas spread with fried black
bean paste and garnished with tomato and green chili salsa. You
can also serve steaks or fillets on a plate, perhaps with some rice
and black beans on the side. Rockfish or other mild white fish
can be served in the same way.

4 shark fillets, 1½ pounds
    total (or 4 steaks, 6 ounces
    each)

Recado Rojo (page 71)

¼ cup vegetable oil

Brush the seasoning paste on all sides of the shark. Set aside to
marinate for several hours in the refrigerator; remove from the
refrigerator half an hour before grilling. Just before grilling, brush
the shark lightly with oil. Grill over a moderately hot charcoal
fire until done by the skewer test (see page 128). Serves 4.

Fresh corn tortillas
are the perfect
accompaniment
for grilled shark.

GRILLED
HALIBUT FLORENTINE

■ ■

This is truly a delightful dish, somewhat lighter than standard "Florentine" preparations. Don't serve it to more than four people at a time, however, as the last-minute maneuvers required could cause the chef to lose his or her cool just before serving time. Above all, this is a dish to savor and relax over. If fresh halibut is not available, make something else for supper; it's just not the same with frozen.

Beurre Blanc, page 85

3 bunches spinach

4 fresh halibut steaks or fillet
   portions, 6 to 8 ounces each

Melted butter

Ground white pepper

Paprika

About 2 tablespoons butter

Salt

Freshly grated nutmeg to taste

1 hard-cooked egg, sieved

Prepare *beurre blanc*, substituting half lemon juice for half of the vinegar, if desired. Hold beurre blanc in a Thermos until needed.

Wash the spinach and remove the stems. Rinse the halibut in cold water; pat dry. Brush lightly with melted butter and dust with white pepper and paprika.

Melt the butter in a large frying pan and put the spinach in the pan while it's still wet. Sprinkle lightly with salt and nutmeg. Cook over a moderate fire until the spinach is half wilted; remove the pan from the heat and set aside.

Grill the halibut over the fire until done according to the skewer test, page 128, about 4 minutes per side. Remove the fish from the grill and finish sautéing the spinach (this should only take a minute or two). Divide the spinach into 4 equal servings on individual plates and top with the halibut. Give the beurre blanc a couple of shakes in the Thermos and pour over the fish. Garnish with the sieved egg. Serves 4.

Shellfish

Many kinds of shellfish can be cooked on the grill with excellent results. The ground rules are simple: cook in the shell whenever possible to preserve moisture and flavor, work quickly over high heat, avoid overcooking, and keep sauces and marinades simple to complement the distinctive flavors of shellfish.

The easiest type of shellfish to cook is the crustacean—crab, lobster, shrimp, and prawns. Whenever possible, these should be cooked in the shell (in some cases there is no other practical way). The shell performs many functions: it gives the meat shape, just as it does to the living animal. More important, it protects the meat from the direct heat, absorbing and diffusing it in much the same way as do bones on the underside of a flattened chicken or a rack of lamb. In addition, as the shell cooks, it adds flavor to the meat.

Dungeness crab... one of the Pacific's finest catches.

GRILLED ABALONE STEAKS

■ ■

This is a post-graduate test of your grilling skills—there is no food more unforgiving of overcooking than abalone. But properly cooked, it is one of the tenderest, most delicious seafoods. The trick is to pound the steaks enough to tenderize them, but not until they fall apart, then to just barely heat them through on the hottest fire you can manage. Frozen abalone steaks will do, but by all means try this dish if you are lucky enough to get fresh abalone.

2 tablespoons minced or grated fresh ginger	2 tablespoons peanut or other vegetable oil
¼ cup soy sauce	8 abalone steaks, about ¼ inch thick
¼ cup sake or dry sherry	

Combine the ginger, soy sauce, and wine. Pour half of the mixture into a shallow bowl and combine it with the oil. Pound the abalone steaks (with a mallet, meat pounder, or the side of a heavy cleaver) to about half their original thickness. Dip each pounded steak in the soy-oil marinade and transfer it to a shallow bowl or plate. When all the steaks are pounded, pour any remaining marinade over them. The steaks may be prepared to this point up to several hours ahead and refrigerated; remove from the refrigerator 30 minutes before grilling. Reserve the remaining soy sauce mixture for a dipping sauce.

Build a hot fire on a hibachi or other open grill and preheat the grill thoroughly. Have all of the accompanying dishes ready and the guests at the table before you start grilling. Cook the steaks just until they begin to shrink and curl at the edges, about 20 seconds on a side. Serve immediately with the soy-ginger-sake dipping sauce. Serves 4.

GRILLED DUNGENESS CRAB

■ ■

To grill large crabs, such as the Pacific Dungeness variety, buy them alive and kill them just before cleaning. The yellowish fat is full of flavor, and can be used in a dipping sauce along with a little butter and some of the marinade.

**2 large live Dungeness crabs,
  each 2 pounds or more**

¼ cup olive oil

Salt and pepper

Fresh thyme

4 tablespoons butter

Buy the crabs alive and kill and clean them just before grilling (you can kill them with a knife, but an easier way is to drop them into boiling water for a minute or two). Split the body down the middle, cutting right through the shell, producing 2 halves with legs. Pull off each shell half, pull out and reserve any yellowish or greenish fat in the corners of the shell, and discard the shell. The body of the crab will probably have more bits of fat attached to it; reserve these too. Pull off and discard the gills (the soft gray fingerlike tissues on the upper side of the body), the small jaws at the front of the body, and the "breastplate" on the underside. Rinse away any remaining matter from the body halves, leaving only shell and meat.

Crack each section of the legs and claws with a mallet or sharpening steel. Put the crab halves in a large bowl, toss with the olive oil, salt, pepper, and thyme, and marinate in the refrigerator for up to several hours.

Remove the crabs from the refrigerator at least 15 minutes before grilling. Grill over a hot fire, turning frequently, until the shell is bright red and the exposed meat is opaque and white. Meanwhile, heat the reserved crab fat with the butter in a saucepan on the edge of the grill. Serve the crab with nutcrackers and cocktail forks, the crab butter as a dipping sauce, and plenty of napkins. Serves 4.

VARIATION Use peanut oil for the marinade and add 1 tablespoon each chopped ginger and garlic, 1 or 2 chopped green chilies, and ¼ cup soy sauce. Heat the reserved marinade with the crab fat for a dipping sauce.

GRILLED LOBSTER

■ ■

Buy live eastern lobsters and kill them as for crab, preceding. Split them lengthwise and reserve the greenish liver, or "tomalley," and the blackish roe (if it is a female). Discard the remaining stuff in the cavity and the intestinal tube running down the middle of the tail.

Grill over a hot fire, starting with 5 to 7 minutes of cooking cut side down, then finishing with the cut side up (this way, the shell will retain any juices released by the meat). When the tail meat is opaque, the lobster is done.

Remove the lobster to a heated platter, twist off the claws, and return them to the grill for another 2 to 3 minutes to finish cooking. Heat the tomalley and roe in a little butter for a dipping sauce. A 1- to 2-pound lobster is normally a single serving, but bigger lobsters can feed two.

The eastern lobster is really best without any additional flavorings.

NOTE Both the eastern lobster and the cosmopolitan rock or spiny lobster can be grilled with excellent results. There is some difference in flavor, but the main difference is that the spiny lobster has almost all its meat in the tail, lacking the large claws of the eastern variety.

The smaller, warm-water spiny lobster, with its milder flavor, will benefit by a marinade such as those listed for crab. If you can buy them alive, kill, split, and clean them in the same way as in the preceding recipe. Frozen tails can also be thawed, split, marinated, and grilled, with very good results.

GRILLED SALMON AND SCALLOP BROCHETTES

■ ■

¾ to 1 pound large fresh
  scallops

¾ to 1 pound salmon fillet

Bay leaves (optional)

Olive oil

Salt and pepper

Dried thyme

Beurre Blanc, page 85 (optional)

Pull off the strip of tough, white flesh from the side of each scallop. Cut the salmon into chunks of roughly the same size as the smaller scallops, and cut any especially large scallops in half. Alternate salmon chunks and scallops on skewers, with pieces of bay leaf here and there. Marinate in olive oil seasoned with salt, pepper, and thyme; refrigerate until half an hour before grilling.

Grill over a hot fire until the salmon is just heated through, about 3 or 4 minutes. Serve brochettes just as they come off the grill, or, if a sauce is desired, with *beurre blanc*. Serves 4 as a main course, 8 to 10 as an appetizer.

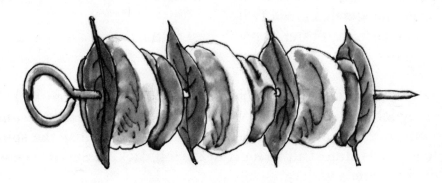

*Beautiful to look at and a delight to eat...
.... skewered salmon and scallops with bay leaves.*

GRILLED SHRIMP
WITH THAI DIPPING SAUCE

■ ■

1½ pounds raw shrimp,
   unpeeled

Peanut oil

Salt and pepper

Thai Sweet and Sour Dipping
   Sauce, page 79

Rinse the shrimp and drain well. Skewer the shrimp by passing a thin skewer through the shell near the head end, then near the tail. Arrange the shrimp brochettes in a shallow pan, drizzle with oil, and sprinkle with salt and pepper. Refrigerate until about 15 minutes before cooking.

Grill the shrimp over the hottest part of the fire until the shells are red and the meat is opaque and white. Serve with the dipping sauce. Small shrimp may be eaten shell and all, but larger shrimp will probably have to be peeled. Serves 6 to 8 as an appetizer, 3 to 4 as a main course.

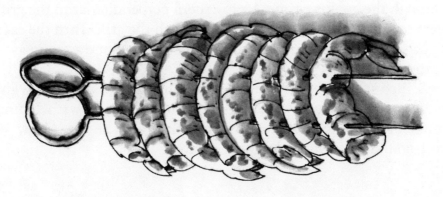

Two skewers make for easy turning on the grill.

And remember not to overcook!

GRILLED SQUID

■ ■

Squid is another type of shellfish that can be delicious grilled, but turns to leather if overcooked. The smaller Pacific species is just the right size for grilling, with a typical size of about 6 inches overall; the larger Atlantic variety tends to be bigger and a little tougher.

The easiest way to grill squid is to cook the sacs whole and the tentacles on skewers. To clean, first cut the tentacles free from the head just beyond the eyes. Squeeze out and discard the beak, a small hard piece in the middle of the tentacles. Grasp the head and pull it out of the sac, drawing out the entrails with it. Pull out the transparent "quill" and rinse out any remaining matter in the sacs. There is no need to remove the purplish outer skin, although you can if you like.

Rinse the tentacles well and skewer them, passing the skewer through the fleshy base. Working over a very hot fire, grill the tentacles about 3 minutes. Add the sacs to the grill halfway through the cooking time, laying them perpendicular to the grill bars to prevent them from falling through the grill. Turn the sacs once with tongs during cooking. The squid is done as soon as it turns opaque.

Grilled squid are delicious without any sauce, but if you want you can serve them with melted butter flavored with lemon juice, or soy sauce flavored with a little grated ginger. Allow ¾ to 1 pound uncleaned squid per person.

GRILLED OYSTERS

■ ■

Oysters are the easiest of the bivalves to cook directly over a fire. Large oysters may be shucked, drained, and cooked on skewers; they will shrink considerably, an advantage if the oysters are especially large. Oysters of any size can be cooked in their shells, or on the half shell. The easiest way is to put the unopened oysters directly on the grill, flat shell up. When the shell pops open, use an oyster knife to remove the top shell, add whatever sauce you are using, and return the half-shell oyster to the grill just long enough to heat the sauce through. If you prefer the oysters just barely cooked, see the following recipe.

TOMALES BAY OYSTER ROAST

■ ■

While the Pacific Coast has no real equivalent of the New England clambake, many of our local shellfish are delicious cooked outdoors over charcoal.

24 large oysters in shells

1 cup butter

6 large garlic cloves, chopped

Juice of 1 lemon

Freshly ground black pepper, or Tabasco or other hot pepper sauce, to taste

1 cup barbecue sauce (pages 74-75)

Scrub the oysters well and store them, flat shell up, in a shallow pan or a bucket until ready to cook. Cover with a damp towel or burlap, but do not store in water.

Prepare a hot fire in an open grill, or a moderate fire in a covered grill. Combine the butter, garlic, and lemon juice in a saucepan and set it to simmer on the edge of the fire.

Just before cooking, open the oysters, remove the flat top shell and cut the oyster loose from the bottom shell (to make it easier to eat). Add a spoonful of the sauce of your choice to each shell— garlic butter with black pepper or Tabasco, or barbecue sauce— and place the oyster on the grill. Cook until the liquid is bubbly and the oyster begins to shrink and curl at the edge. Serve with chilled dry white wine or beer and French bread. Serves 4.

Vegetables

Grilled vegetables are an excellent addition to an outdoor meal. A wide range of vegetables can be cooked directly over a charcoal fire. Some can be grilled as is, while others require some preliminary cooking in the kitchen.

Novice vegetable grillers will probably want to start with onions and leeks. After all, a grilled slice of red or yellow onion is a familiar enough adjunct to a hamburger. Trimmed whole scallions make an excellent garnish for grilled fish steaks or fillets. Leeks are also delicious grilled and, if small enough, need no preliminary cooking.

Look for the largest scallions for a pungent grilled treat.

Depending on the length of time on the grill, the outside surfaces of vegetables may or may not be charred. Grilling whole peppers is a convenient way to remove the waxy skin; in fact, even if you are not serving peppers with the meal, you can take advantage of the early stage of your fire by roasting some peppers for future use. The outer skin of whole garlic heads or onions usually burns, but peeling away the charred parts reveals the delicious roasted interior. Grilling corn on the cob in its husk gives the same effect, allowing the corn to cook without browning; but if you prefer, you can grill the husked ears, which gives the corn a more pronounced flavor.

Vegetables that cook relatively quickly are the best for direct grilling. Zucchini and other summer squashes are a natural for summer meals, as are slices of fresh, ripe tomatoes. Green tomatoes are even easier to grill in slices, and their tart flavor makes for an interesting side dish. Slices of eggplant, or halves of the slender Asian varieties, are another good choice for the grill; the dry heat of the charcoal fire allows you to cook them without the horrendous quantities of oil needed for sautéed eggplant dishes. (Of course, you may want to use some olive oil for flavor. A light brushing of seasoned oil while the eggplant cooks is sufficient.) For a lighter interpretation of eggplant Parmesan, try serving grilled slices with a freshly made tomato sauce, topped with grated Parmigiano or Asiago cheese.

Some of the denser vegetables require a preliminary cooking before finishing them on the grill. Cut-up potatoes, sweet potatoes, and yams can all be grilled with excellent results; steam or boil them until almost done, marinate briefly in oil, and grill until the outside is browned and crisp. Artichokes are another pleasant surprise on the grill; prepare them as you would for pickling, in halves, quarters, or wedges according to size, but finish them on the grill for an unusual accompaniment to grilled meats.

The hinged grill is helpful when grilling sliced vegetables. See the accompanying box for other grilled vegetable ideas.

The humble carrot takes on a new dimension when grilled over charcoal.

VEGETABLES FOR GRILLING

Artichokes Halves, quarters, wedges. Parboil and marinate in pieces before grilling.

Carrots Thick slices or sticks. Blanch before grilling.

Celery Whole stalks or sticks.

Corn On the cob, with or without husks. Can also be cooked in foil or in husks on the grill, or directly in the ashes.

Cucumbers Split or quarters; peeled, salted, and drained.

Eggplants Whole if very small, slices or halves if larger.

Fennel Halves or slices; may be blanched to speed cooking.

Garlic Whole heads; discard outer skin after cooking.

Jícama Thin slices; interesting only if eaten immediately.

Leeks Split if large, whole if small. May be blanched first if large.

Mushrooms Cultivated: skewered through stem and cap; blanching helpful to prevent cracking. Wild: sliced caps if large, skewered if smaller. Dried black *(shiitake):* soak, remove stems; grill whole caps.

Onions Whole or halved; remove charred skin after grilling. Scallions: Whole.

Peppers Whole; remove charred skin, seeds, veins after cooking. May also be cut up raw for brochettes.

Potatoes Parboil or steam, drain well, oil, and grill in quarters or slices.

Rhubarb Whole stalks.

Summer Squashes Whole if very small, split or sliced if larger.

Sweet Potatoes, Yams Same as potatoes.

Tomatoes Whole or thick slices. Skewer very small types.

CORN
GRILLED IN ITS LEAVES

■ ■

4 ears fresh sweet corn

¼ cup butter, softened

Salt and pepper to taste

1 teaspoon ancho or
New Mexico chili powder
(optional)

Peel back the leaves of each ear of corn, but leave them attached
at the base. Remove all of the corn silk. Combine the butter and
seasonings and rub the mixture lightly all over the corn. Fold the
leaves back up around the corn. Tie the tops of the leaves
together with string or a strip of one of the outside leaves.

Grill over a hot to moderate fire until the outer leaves are
charred, 10 to 15 minutes. Guests should peel corn over plates,
to catch any dripping butter. Pass any remaining chili butter.
Serves 4.

*If you've
never tried corn
grilled in the
husk, you've
missed one of the
unique flavors
of summer.*

GRILLED
ARTICHOKE QUARTERS

■ ■

Choose large, meaty artichokes to get the greatest yield for the amount of work.

1 lemon, cut in half

1 pound artichokes (2 to 4, depending on size)

Olive oil

Salt and pepper

Have a bowl of acidulated water (water plus the juice of half the lemon) ready. Starting with the outermost leaves of an artichoke, bend each leaf backwards until it snaps off near the base, Discard the leaves. Every minute or so, stop and rub the freshly broken surface of the artichoke with the cut lemon (to prevent discoloration). Continue breaking off leaves, and work your way toward the top of the artichoke. When the exposed leaves show more yellow than green, remove and discard the whole green top of the artichoke, then cut the base into quarters. Rub the cut surfaces with lemon. With a small knife, remove the fuzzy choke and the tiny inner leaves. You will be left with the fleshy part of the artichoke: the stem, bottom, and the thick bases of the outer leaves. Drop each quarter into the acidulated water as you finish.

Bring an ample pot of salted water to a boil. Parboil the cleaned artichoke quarters until they are cooked through but not mushy, then drain and marinate in olive oil seasoned with salt and pepper until ready to grill. Grill over a moderate fire until lightly browned. Serves 4 to 6.

*artichoke...
the edible
thistle.*

MIXED VEGETABLE BROCHETTES

■ ■

Mixed skewers of meat and vegetables are attractive, but they do not always cook at the same rate. Another alternative is to cook an assortment of vegetables on separate skewers and serve perfectly cooked vegetables alongside perfectly cooked meats. Choose an assortment of the following:

Red or green peppers, seeded and deveined, in 1-inch squares

Button mushrooms, skewered sideways through the cap

Sweet onions (especially Vidalia, Walla Walla, or Maui), in 1-inch cubes

Zucchini, sliced 1 inch thick and skewered through the skin so the cut side faces the grill

Cherry or yellow pear tomatoes

Eggplant, in 1-inch cubes

Artichoke hearts or bottoms, canned, or as prepared in recipe on page 154

Olive oil

Salt and pepper to taste

Dried thyme or oregano (optional)

Combine the vegetables in an attractive pattern on thin skewers, using firmer vegetables such as onions and peppers to support more fragile ones like tomatoes and mushrooms. Marinate briefly in olive oil with salt, pepper, and perhaps dried thyme or oregano. Grill over a moderate fire until the onions and peppers are soft but not charred.

Look for the big sweet ones.

GRILLED
CHEESE-STUFFED PEPPERS

■ ■

Try this adaptation of *chiles rellenos* as a side dish with grilled steaks or pork chops.

4 large green chilies (the dark green chile poblano, also known as chile pasilla, is the best; otherwise use the long green Anaheim variety)

3 medium-sized tomatoes

Salt and pepper

1 cup coarsely grated jack cheese

Oil

While the fire is in its early, flaming stage, roast the whole peppers, turning as necessary until the skins are evenly blistered and blackening, and roast the tomatoes until the skins begin to brown. Transfer the chilies to a plastic or paper bag, seal tightly, and let them "sweat" until soft, 15 minutes or so. Transfer the tomatoes to a shallow dish, chop them roughly (skins and all) with a metal spoon, and season to taste with salt and pepper.

When the peppers are cool enough to handle, peel away the charred outer skin. Make a lengthwise cut in each pepper and remove the seeds and as much of the veins as possible, leaving the stem end attached. Stuff each pepper gently with cheese, fold the cut ends together, and seal up the cut with a toothpick or two.

Oil the stuffed peppers lightly and grill them alongside the meat until the cheese is melted, about 8 minutes, and serve with the chopped tomatoes as a sauce. Serves 4 as a side dish, 2 as a main dish.

GRILLED RATATOUILLE

■■■■■■■■■■■■■■■■■■■■■■■■■

Ratatouille, the famous dish of southern France made with egg-plant and other summer vegetables, is usually cooked on the stove, but a delicious version can be done outdoors on the grill. The vegetables cook separately during the early stage of the fire, and are then combined with oil and herbs to marinate while the main course is on the grill.

The amounts and proportions of the vegetables are less impor-tant than the basic procedure: if you like zucchini more than eggplant, feel free to use more zucchini; if you like hotter flavors, use green chilies or hot Italian peppers, and so on. The only rule is that the combination should be colorful and taste great. Each vegetable should be cooked enough to be tender and give some of its juices to the dish, but not so much that it becomes mushy and loses its identity.

1 whole head of garlic

3 small or 2 large yellow or red onions

½ pound red, yellow, or green peppers

1 pound ripe tomatoes

1 pound eggplant, Asian or Mediterranean type

¾ pound summer squash (zucchini, yellow crookneck, scallop, or an assortment)

½ cup good, fruity olive oil

Salt and pepper

½ teaspoon dried oregano or marjoram

2 tablespoons chopped fresh herbs (basil, chives, parsley, thyme)

Have a large bowl and a cutting board available. As soon as some parts of the fire are getting hot, you can begin cooking the vegetables in the following order, adding more items as grill space becomes available.

- Cook the whole garlic until the outside skin is charred and the cloves feel tender. Remove the whole head to the board, let cool enough to handle, and separate the cloves. Cut open each clove and squeeze the flesh into the bowl.

- Split the onions lengthwise and grill until the outside skins and cut sides are charred. Peel and scrape away the charred portions, slice the onions about ⅛ inch thick, and add to the bowl.

- Cook the whole peppers over the hottest part of the fire until the skins are evenly blackened. Remove them from the grill to a plastic or paper bag, to let them steam. When the peppers have cooled somewhat, peel away all of the charred skin, remove the stems, seeds, and veins, and cut the peppers into strips. Add them to the bowl.

- Grill the tomatoes until the skins are blackened in spots, but the flesh is still fairly firm. Cut the tomatoes, skins and all, into quarters or wedges and add them to the bowl.

- Slice the eggplant lengthwise, up to ½ inch thick. Brush the slices very lightly with oil and grill until tender, moving the slices around on the grill as necessary to prevent scorching. If using small Asian eggplants, add the slices whole to the bowl, otherwise cut the slices into smaller, bite-sized pieces.

- Split the summer squash lengthwise into halves if small, or thick slices if larger. Grill just until tender and add to the bowl.

Sprinkle the oil, salt, pepper, oregano, and herbs over the vegetables in the bowl and toss lightly to combine thoroughly. Let the mixture marinate while the rest of the meal is cooking, and serve at room temperature. Serves 6 to 8 as a side dish.

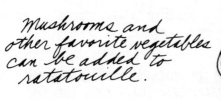
Mushrooms and other favorite vegetables can be added to ratatouille.

GRILLED POTATO WEDGES

■ ■

Try this unusual variation on the meat-and-potatoes theme with any grilled meats. The potato wedges can slip into the spaces between steaks, chops, or burgers on the grill to cook at the same time. The potatoes can be prepared well ahead of time, making this a good picnic item.

Cut 4 large new potatoes (white or red) lengthwise into 4 to 6 wedges each. Steam the potatoes until tender but not too soft. Transfer the potato wedges to a shallow dish; sprinkle them with olive oil, salt, and pepper. Toss the potatoes to cover them evenly with oil and set aside until ready to grill. Cook the potato wedges over a moderate to hot fire until lightly browned. Drizzle with a little more olive oil after cooking, if desired. Serves 4.

GRILLED POTATO SKINS

■ ■

Grilled potato skins are great served with steaks, ribs, or chops. They are hearty fare, meant to be slathered with butter, chives, sour cream, and plenty of pepper. Once you've had potatoes this way, you may never go back to plain old baked potatoes; who needs the insides, anyway?

Follow the directions for Baked Potatoes, page 160. When the potatoes are just tender (about 1 hour), remove from the oven. Slit open and remove all but about ¼ inch of the flesh (which can be saved for potato pancakes, soup, or hashed browns), then flatten the whole potato skin closed with the palm of your hand.

Place the flattened skins on the grill at the same time as the rest of your meal. They should be turned, and grilled long enough to make the skin crispy on both sides. Some people are so crazy about these that you might plan on serving 2 per person.

The following foods are not cooked on the grill, but they are considered by many to be almost indispensable side dishes to serve with grilled foods.

BAKED POTATOES

■ ■

The baked potato continues to be one of the best accompaniments for grilled food, especially beef. These instructions are for real baked-potato lovers, because real baked potato lovers always eat the peel as well as the insides. And there's nothing worse than a baked potato that's only partially cooked, or one with a soggy skin.

Preheat the oven to 375°F. Start with 4 (or however many you need) brown-skinned baking potatoes. Wash and scrub the skins in cold water; poke a few holes in each with a fork. Do not, under any circumstances, wrap the potatoes in aluminum foil. Place the potatoes in the middle of the upper rack of the oven. One hour is the minimum amount of time it takes to produce a potato with an acceptably crunchy skin. If you find that the rest of your meal is not ready when the potatoes have been the oven for 60 minutes, do not turn the oven down. Once the temperature has been turned down, the potatoes will start to emit steam, and there goes the crunchy skin. No, it's far better to err on the side of extra crunchy than to wind up with soggy, steamed potato skins. Cut open, and go heavy on the butter, sour cream, chives or chopped scallion tops, salt, and freshly ground pepper, and resolve to start that diet first thing in the morning.

POMMES FRITES

■ ■

French-fried potatoes, or *pommes frites*, are delicious with almost any simple grilled food. Double-frying is the "secret" to exemplary results. Wash and scrub 4 large, long white potatoes in cold water, but do not peel. Cut by hand, using a sharp knife, into uniform ⅜-inch square sticks, 3 to 4 inches long, or use a food processor.

In a deep, heavy pan, heat at least 4 cups of oil to 300°F and cook in approximately 3 even batches for 4 or 5 minutes each. Do not let the potatoes brown; the first frying phase is to partially cook or soften the potatoes. Remove the potatoes with a slotted spoon, or use a wire basket if you have one, and place on a cookie sheet lined with several thicknesses of paper toweling. At this point the potatoes can be held at room temperature for 3 or 4 hours, or overnight, loosely covered, in the refrigerator.

When you are ready to serve them, reheat the oil to 375°F and cook the potatoes again in 3 even batches, for approximately 3 minutes, or until they are a light golden brown. Remove from the oil with a slotted spoon, drain, and pour into a napkin-lined basket. Sprinkle with salt to taste. Serves 4.

SHOESTRING POTATOES

■ ■

Shoestring potatoes—the preferred choice by many to accompany grilled fish—are not that difficult to make at home. Count on "shoe-stringing" 1 large potato per person. Wash and scrub 4 large baking potatoes in cold water, but do not peel. Slice the potatoes using a mandoline (see below) set at slightly less than ⅛-inch thick. Drop the shoestrings into a bowl of cold water. (Note: There's no need to acidulate the water, using vinegar or lemon juice, or to add salt; the water may turn brown, but the potatoes won't.) Drain and spin dry (using a salad spinner), or blot well with paper towels.

(continued)

An old-fashioned mandoline makes quick work of a mountain of potatoes.

Heat at least 4 cups of oil in a heavy, deep pan to 375°F. (Note: An electric pressure cooker, if you have one, works well for this process; simply set the thermostat to 375°F and use without the lid.) Add the potatoes to the hot oil in approximately 3 even batches. Cook for 3 minutes, or until they are a light golden brown; remove with a slotted spoon. Drain and pour into a napkin-lined basket. Sprinkle with salt to taste. Serves 4.

ROSTI POTATOES

■■■■■■■■■■■■■■■■■■■■■■

Rösti potatoes are a perfect accompaniment for both fish and meat dishes. Because they require some last-minute preparation, it's a good idea to plan a meal that can stand to wait a few minutes while you finish the potatoes.

4 or 5 large brown-skinned baking potatoes	**Salt and pepper**
½ cup butter	**Minced parsley**

Wash the potatoes and place them in a large pot with water to cover. Boil the potatoes for approximately 15 minutes, until slightly tender. Drain, cool, and peel the potatoes. Coarsely grate the potatoes using a hand-held grater or a food processor with a coarse grating attachment.

Melt 2 or 3 tablespoons of the butter in a large, well-seasoned cast-iron skillet (or one with a relatively nonstick surface) over medium-high heat. Add the grated potatoes and press down to create an even layer. Sprinkle with salt and freshly ground pepper to taste and dot with 2 more tablespoons of the butter. Using a spatula, lift a corner of this giant potato "pancake" to see if it has turned a golden brown; this usually takes 8 to 10 minutes. Place a large plate (larger than the skillet by a couple of inches) on top of the skillet and turn the skillet and plate upside down. Slip the "pancake" back into the skillet, uncooked side down, dot with the remaining butter, and continue to cook until golden brown.

Cut in wedges and serve straight from the pan, or do the inverted pan and plate trick again and serve from the table. Sprinkle with parsley. Serves 4.

POTATOES CHEVALIER

■ ■

This recipe is a distinguished variation of Potatoes Anna, as developed by the chatelaine of Château Chevalier (with all the ingredients freshly gathered from a magnificent vegetable garden). These potatoes are absolutely delicious with grilled lamb (pages 95 and 98) or any grilled beef.

4 large baking potatoes

3 tablespoons butter

3 tablespoons olive or vegetable oil

3 or 4 garlic cloves, minced or pressed

4 tablespoons chopped fresh tarragon, or 2 teaspoons dried tarragon

Salt and pepper

Chopped fresh tarragon or parsley

Preheat the oven to 400°F. Wash and peel the potatoes; slice evenly into $\frac{3}{16}$-inch slices. Melt the butter and oil in a large, heavy skillet (with a cover). Add the garlic and cook for 30 seconds. Add the potatoes, tarragon, salt, and pepper to taste. Mix the potatoes around to coat evenly with the butter, oil, and herb mixture. After coating, try to arrange the potatoes in overlapping concentric circles, one layer on top of another. If this is just too much to ask, don't worry; what is lost in aesthetics will not be lost in flavor. Put the cover on the pan and slip it into the oven for approximately 45 minutes. After 45 minutes, remove the lid, and continue baking until the potatoes start to brown on top— another 10 or 15 minutes. When the potatoes are nice and tender, have a large plate (larger than the skillet by a couple of inches) ready. Place the plate on top of the skillet, hold it in place, and turn upside down. Sprinkle with extra chopped tarragon or parsley and whisk to the table. Cut into wedges. Serves 4.

Cheese and Bread

Once you have gone to the trouble of building a charcoal fire, it seems a shame not to use it for as many parts of the meal as possible. Why not use the fire to toast the bread, or for that matter, why not add a warm cheese course?

Most grillers are familiar with one form of grilled bread— toasted hamburger buns. But any good bread can be toasted over the fire, and a crusty French loaf tastes especially good. If you are grilling meats for a filling for tacos, burritos, or Souvlaki Pita (page 100), you can also use the same fire to warm these breads.

Bruschetta is the general name for a variety of grilled breads from Italy. The basic bruschetta on page 165 (known as *fettunta* in some parts of Italy) may be the original garlic bread, and we think it is far superior to the usual paprika-cheese-butter variety. Another bruschetta (page 166) is actually a dessert, with cheese and honey.

For grilling, a crusty, fresh loaf is best.

GRILLED CHEESES

■ ■

Grilling cheese is easy when it is on top of a slice of bread or a hamburger, but you can also grill some cheeses all by themselves. If your grill bars are close together, thoroughly clean, and well seasoned, try grilling a slice of young Parmesan-type cheese until it becomes slightly browned and bubbly on the edges. A flat disc of firm goat cheese, either plain or marinated in olive oil with herbs and pepper, becomes especially aromatic and delicious when briefly heated on the grill. (If your grill surface is not ideal, try grilling the cheese on top of a washed and oiled piece of metal screen.)

BRUSCHETTA
Charcoal-Grilled Garlic Bread

■ ■

Thanks to Maggie Klein (author of *The Feast of the Olive* [Berkeley, California: Aris Books, 1983]), for inspiring this recipe for *bruschetta*, arguably the original form of garlic bread. She considers it winter food, to be enjoyed by the fire with the year's brand-new pressing of olive oil, but we find that the exuberant flavors of garlic and olive oil fit in perfectly with outdoor cooking and eating any time of year. Bruschetta makes an ideal appetizer, giving the hungry family or guests something to eat while your fire is getting to the perfect point for cooking the entrée.

Italian or French bread,
  preferably homemade

Whole peeled garlic cloves
  (approximately 1 clove for
  each 2 or 3 slices of bread)

Extra-virgin olive oil

Salt and pepper (optional)

Slice the bread into thick slices (baguettes may be split lengthwise) and toast on the grill. Immediately rub the warm toasts with a clove of garlic impaled on a fork. (If you are serving a large group, simply cut a well-peeled head of garlic in half and rub that over the bread.) Drizzle with plenty of oil and season with salt and pepper, if you like.

BRUSCHETTA
WITH CHEESE AND HONEY

■ ■

This dish was inspired by a favorite dessert at Badia a Coltibuono, an eleventh-century Italian abbey that is now a private estate producing traditional Tuscan products including wine, olive oil, and an intriguing range of honeys. Piero Stucchi-Prinetti and his wife Lorenza de Medici create a simple and delicious dessert of grilled *pecorino toscano* cheese and honey from the estate's chestnut trees. This adaptation puts the same combination on a slice of toast, moistened with a good, fruity olive oil. Unfortunately, *pecorino toscano*, a firm, slightly tangy sheep's milk cheese, is not available here; the closest equivalent is *pecorino sardo*, from Sardinia, and even that is uncommon. The widely distributed *pecorino romano* is definitely not the same. Asiago works well, or Italian Fontina, or even Gruyère. Be sure to use a first-rate olive oil and a flavorful honey.

Italian or French bread,
    preferably homemade

Extra-virgin olive oil

Asiago, Fontina, or Gruyère
    cheese, in thick slices

Honey, preferably with a strong
    flower or herb flavor

Cut the bread into ¾-inch slices. Toast lightly on one side over a moderate fire. Turn, and while the other side is toasting, drizzle generously with olive oil and top with a layer of cheese. Continue toasting until the cheese melts, moving the toasts to a cooler part of the fire if necessary to keep from burning. Serve the toasts on small plates and let each person top his or her piece with honey.

SPECIALITES DE
Legendary
CAFE PROMETHEUS*

Author A. Cort Sinnes in a rare photograph of the legendary Café Prometheus dining room.

The Café Prometheus sits approximately two-thirds of the way up Mount Saint Helena (which everyone hopes is an inactive volcano), overlooking the Napa Valley, California's premier grape and wine-producing region.

The Prometheus is not far from where Robert Louis Stevenson spent his honeymoon in an abandoned silver mine called Silverado. It is a part of the world rich in history and tradition, with the Prometheus figuring prominently in many local legends and tales. The turnoff is not marked on the road, but a well-worn gravel driveway dips down into a stand of Douglas fir and madrone from which emanates an eerie glow created by the

*Any resemblance Café Prometheus might have to any existing restaurant is purely coincidental.   PHOTOGRAPH BY ROLAND DARE

pinkish neon sign on the side of the nondescript building, spelling out "The Café Prometheus" in a rather loose script, situated directly above a snappy canvas marquee. Although it is unusual in such a rural setting, there's always a parking attendant there to open your door and take the car away to some unknown location. Because there is no parking lot, it's difficult to tell how many patrons will be present on any given evening, but year in and year out, there always seems to be enough activity to give the place an air of festivity and warmth.

Bernard, the legendary and inscrutable *maître d'*, is always on hand in the small, damask-curtained vestibule, ready with a knowing nod, and a "right this way, Mr. So-and-So," and the evening begins.

The perfectly lit dining room and bar look like a cross between a tidy *belle époque* bordello and the splendid rustic retreat of some long-dead robber baron. It is a low-ceilinged room, adorned with gilt-framed California landscapes from the turn of the century. Each table is covered with perfectly pressed white linen, embroidered rather conspicuously with the Prometheus insignia, as are the napkins, which themselves could double for small tablecloths. A silver candlestick, topped with a small pleated pink silk shade, adorns each table, diffusing a light like that of the sun seen from the inside of a shell. Heavy plated dinner-sized silver is set out, each piece engraved with a small depiction of Prometheus. In the center of the room there is always an extraordinary, enormous bouquet of seasonal flowers, arranged by Bernard himself and cut from his sizable home flower garden, down the hill in Calistoga. If you want to see Bernard's normally steady eyes light up, ask him about his delphiniums or his four-foot-tall foxtail lilies.

Surprisingly in such a renowned wine-producing region, dinners here almost always start with a cocktail or two, expertly crafted by Einar the bartender, who spent twenty years shipboard with Cunard before "retiring" to the Prometheus. One of the most unusual things about the Café Prometheus is the fact that all the crystal is indeed crystal; Baccarat, in fact. When questioned about such an extravagant touch, Bernard states flatly that "having a bit of breakable perfection on the table helps to add a certain level of decorum, a little like inviting a stranger to a family dinner; it helps keep the situation under control."

A little something to snack on during cocktails might be the ethereal deep-fried calamari or the fried cheese (delicious with chilled champagne), brought to your table folded deep within white linen, or a good selection of fresh oysters, or perhaps a little Nova Scotia salmon. Nothing particularly fancy, but everything you'd want, and all of it perfectly fresh and painstakingly presented.

There are no menus, just a recital from your waiter; besides, just about everyone who goes there knows what they want before sitting down, and if, perchance, that selection is not available, there is always an agreeable substitution. Aged choice beef, veal chops, an array of fresh fish and shellfish, and rack of lamb, all cooked over a hot mesquite grill, are among the favorites. About ten different types of potatoes — from skins to shoestrings — are offered, as well as the standard vegetable mélange, a sort of *ratatouille* that changes with the seasons. Fresh sourdough French bread is always present, trucked up from San Francisco. The hearts of palm or endive and watercress salad is highly recommended, served in just the right portions. Homemade desserts, made for the past thirty years by Margaret, who drives all the way from Middletown four times a week, are the kind that maybe mother didn't even make: bread pudding with whiskey sauce, fantastic fresh berry pies redolent with grated nutmeg, and a custard that goes down, in Margaret's words, "like the Lord in silk pajamas."

Now if this sounds like the menu from just another traditional grill restaurant, I guess that's what it probably is. But there is something about the best ingredients, expertly but simply prepared, that transcends what is currently fashionable and goes directly to the heart of the dining experience. After all, one doesn't really want to be dazzled by the dexterity of a chef or the complexity of his or her dishes (unless one has become severely jaded) so much as to be nourished, in the true sense of the word. So the next time you're in the mood for a little old-fashioned nourishment presented in faultless style, see if you can't find the legendary Café Prometheus; it's right over there. You can't miss it if you keep your eyes open for an eerie pink glow, in a stand of firs, on the side of Mount Saint Helena, the sleeping guardian of the Napa Valley.

In addition to offering sophisticated grilled fare, the Café Prometheus serves up the old standbys—steaks, ribs, chicken, and hamburgers—in an exemplary fashion. The following recipes are adapted from the Café kitchen to home grilling equipment, and help to elevate pedestrian fare to legendary status.

PROMETHEAN CHICKEN

■ ■

In this "recipe," the secret to success is not the ingredients so much as the technique. Any whole or cut-up fresh frying chicken will do, with any combination of flavor enhancers—dry or liquid marinade, basting sauce, or what have you—that suits your mood. Remember, though, if you're going to use a marinade that includes tomato sauce, catsup, sugar, or honey, wipe it off as best you can before putting the chicken on the grill. By the same token, if you are using a basting sauce that contains any of the aforementioned ingredients, don't apply it until the last 5 or so minutes of the time that any one basted side is turned toward the coals. Any deviation from these rules will almost certainly result in chicken with a coat of burned sauce (actually it's the sugar that caramelizes and then burns quickly in the presence of high heat).

The technique, then, is as follows:

1. Use a covered grill. Clean the ashes out of the bottom, start the fire, and clean the grill.

2. When the fire has died down from very hot to hot, put the chicken on the grill, directly over the coals, skin

side down. If you are using cut-up chicken, place the breasts towards the outside of the grill—partly directly over the coals and partly not. Work somewhat quickly so that you can get the cover on the grill before the fat starts to render and create flames. The bottom draft holes should be completely open; the top, three-quarters open.

3. In 7 to 10 minutes close the bottom drafts completely and lift off the lid. If you don't close the bottom draft, the sudden influx of oxygen will start an immediate fire from the accumulated renderings. By closing off the bottom draft, you delay this reaction, at least long enough to turn the chicken. If you did not clean out the ashes from the bottom of the grill before starting, the combination of closing the bottom draft and pulling off the cover will create a suction effect, drawing ashes up to your chicken. Return the cover after turning the chicken, and completely open the bottom draft again.

4. Repeat the procedure in 7 to 10 minutes. At this point you may add basting sauce to the chicken. Turn the chicken in 5 minutes, using the procedure outlined above; wait 5 minutes, and baste the other side again. In short, you've grilled the unbasted chicken for 8 to 10 minutes per side, and basted the chicken twice on one side, and once on the other, 5 minutes per side, for a total cooking time of approximately 25 minutes. Serve and eat as soon as possible—hot off the grill!

PROMETHEAN RIBS

■ ■

At the Café Prometheus, the ribs are always pork ribs, although you may feel free to use this same method with beef ribs. If you use pork, however, do not under any circumstances fall prey to the misconception that you are doing anything beneficial by "parboiling" the ribs before cooking. Frankly we think the horrors of trichinosis would be preferable to the taste of pork meat that has been partially cooked in boiling, fatty water—really, now! That admonition aside, the procedure for cooking excellent ribs is identical to chicken, with the exception of a slightly longer cooking time: 10 to 12 minutes per side, then 3 brushings with basting sauce at 5 minutes per side, for a total cooking time of approximately 40 minutes.

At the Café Prometheus, Chef Cole liberally dusts the ribs, an hour or so prior to cooking, with paprika, freshly ground pepper, garlic powder, and a little commercially prepared "seasoned salt" (which he keeps concealed from view, lest any passersby should think he has sold out and gone "commercial").

Just before putting the ribs on the grill, Chef Cole adds a handful or two of damp hickory or mesquite wood shavings to the edges of the coals for an extra aromatic touch. The basting sauce — which incidentally, is mopped on liberally during the last 15 minutes of cooking time — is very similar to the one found on page 75.

Use a sharp cleaver to chop up the ribs, and provide big napkins to mop up the hands and faces of the satisfied diners.

PROMETHEAN STEAK

■ ■

Even people who consistently dine on fish or chicken occasionally find it hard to resist what M.F.K. Fisher referred to as "a mechanical blast of protein" — the classic beef steak. If your beef eating is occasional, it might as well be great, so be sure and treat yourself to the best possible meat you can procure — usually restaurant-quality well-aged U.S.D.A. Choice or Prime.

Chef Cole says to be sure and let the meat come to room temperature before grilling, and dust with coarsely ground pepper, straight from the mill; do not salt. (It can be a delight to the eye, for those who enjoy such things, to place the steaks on an attractive platter, garnished with a couple of parsley sprigs, where they can be admired before cooking.)

An uncovered grill works best for steaks, with the grill approximately 3 inches from a hot fire. Before placing the steaks on the grill, rub it with a piece of fat trimmed from the steak, stuck on the end of a fork. For an 1½-inch thick steak over a hot fire, you should be able to cook the steaks to medium-rare perfection in 2 turns of approximately 5 to 6 minutes per side. Pull the steaks off the grill in a flash, place a dollop of Chef Cole's Roquefort butter (following) on top, and watch the gods smile.

ROQUEFORT BUTTER

■ ■

Blend 2 ounces of French Roquefort cheese, 6 tablespoons of unsalted butter, and 1 minced garlic clove together to form a smooth mixture. Makes ½ cup, enough for 4 steaks.

PROMETHEAN HAMBURGER

■ ■

The Café grinds its own beef chuck daily. Given the time, when making an occasional hamburger for himself, Chef Cole prefers to chop the meat by hand with a large chef's knife, mincing a third of a pound or so of cubes of chuck in about 45 seconds of high-speed chopping. He then forms the patty *gently* (as it is done with the machine-ground meat for the customers) into a disc an inch thick. He only handles the meat enough to shape it and smooth the surface. To grill it medium rare, his preference, he cooks it on a hot part of the grill, 5 minutes on the first side and about 3 minutes on the second side. Testing it with the end of the spatula blade to tell when it is done, he pulls it off the grill when the top is slightly springy, and places it on an onion roll briefly toasted on the grill. You will never see a cook at CP pressing hard on a cooking hamburger with the spatula, a trick used by "hack cooks in greasy-spoon diners to get the excess fat out of lousy meat," in Chef Cole's words.

Home cooks who are comfortable chopping meat by hand may want to try this technique, but a food processor makes it even easier. Start with cubes of not-too-lean chuck — if about 10 percent of what you see is fat, the proportion is about right. Too little fat will make a dry hamburger, if cooked anywhere beyond rare. If you prefer to buy your meat already ground, choose the middle range of fat content, not the extra-lean variety. In any case, form the burgers gently and don't mess with them too much on the grill. One pound of chuck will serve 3.

CHAPTER FIVE

PRIMEVAL CUISINE: CLAMBAKES AND CAMPFIRES

For all its innovations, today's grill cooking can be legitimately seen as a substitute for the joys of cooking freshly caught food in the great outdoors. Let's face it, clambakes and campfires are at the heart of grilling. The point of this chapter, aside from giving you information on how to have a few spectacular outdoor feasts, is that a great deal can be added to grilling at home if you know what you're imitating in the first place.

So come outdoors with us for a while. We'll start at the beach and work our way into the mountains.

CLAMBAKES

■▪■▪■▪■▪■▪■▪■▪■▪■▪■▪■▪■▪■▪■▪■▪■▪■▪■▪■▪■

Clambakes have been an integral part of beach picnics on the East Coast for as long as anyone can remember. The following excerpt, from *Camp Cookery—How to Live in Camp*, written by Miss M. Parloa, was published by the Graves, Locke and Company in Boston in 1878. The preface states: "In preparing this little book my aim has been to give only dishes that any gentleman, be he ever so ignorant of the most common dish, will have no difficulty in cooking for himself or friends."

Miss Parloa's directions for a clambake are as helpful today as they were over a hundred years ago. Herewith, Miss Parloa on the subject of a clambake:

> For a party of from ten to twenty persons,—First, make an oven of flat stones placed together in the form of a square, on a flat surface about two and a half feet square; around the edge of these, place other stones to form a bin. Fill this oven with small kindlings, such as can be gathered on the beach. On these, pile a few armfuls of larger sticks, crosswise, so that the top can be well covered with stones about the size of one's two hands. Start the fire, and allow it to burn down until the stones, which were on top of the wood, settle down into the oven. Clean out all the cinders with a poker or stick; for, if allowed to remain, the smoke from them will spoil the bake. This must be done very quickly, that the oven may not cool. Cover the oven with fresh seaweed about an inch and one-half thick. On the seaweed, spread the clams so the vegetables, &c., may be placed on top of them: then, in order, put on onions, sweet or Irish potatoes, or both, green corn, then the (blue or cod) fish, and a live lobster, if one can be had; if not, a boiled one, which will be very nice warmed up in this way.
>
> Every thing to be used should be close at hand, to be put on the oven rapidly while it is very hot. Cover the whole bake with a piece of cheap cotton cloth, to keep out dirt; then cover all with seaweed until no steam escapes Bake thirty-five minutes. Remove the covering from one corner at a time only,—so that the rest may keep hot,—and all hands fall to, and help themselves. It is nice eaten with drawn butter or vinegar and pepper.

To Prepare the Fish, Vegetables, &c. — A party of ten to twenty will require a bushel of clams, which should be washed in two or more waters (*fresh water*; salt water will not remove the fine sand); have ready a basket close at hand, as soon as the oven is hot. Clean the fish nicely, split the backs, season with salt and white pepper, and wrap in a clean cloth; wash the potatoes clean, and cut the ends off; husk the corn, leaving the inner layer to keep it clean.

What does a Californian know about clambakes? Admittedly, they are not part of the typical western heritage, but any geographic region with access to a beach has its own form of beach cookery. The following piece by California's M. F. K. Fisher gives a westerner's view of seaside grilling.

THE BEACHERS

— M. F. K. Fisher

Beachers are people who like to eat on beaches.

Some people do not: perhaps cold sand, blowing sand, sand in pants and shoes. . . beachers do, perhaps perversely. They feel more alive if they are "down there," even if their fire goes out and the beer is charged with what gritty stuff has not already stuck to the hot steak sandwiches. They feel alive on the beach.

As a beacher from the age of about four years, I feel qualified to talk about others of my persuasion, and I find from them that there are a couple of things that seem to make beach-eating not only a natural ceremony but an almost atavistic necessity. First, the beach must be as free as possible from other humanoids. Second, a fire, no matter how small and flickering, is not essential but is eminently desirable, especially after sundown. (An apple or a sandwich can be good in daylight, but with the dark the flames make for reassurance. . . .)

California and the whole western coastline offer hundreds of miles of coves, stretches, bays, inlets, delta-sands, for the primeval right of building a fire and then heating food over it in the privacy that is both animal and overtly cleansing to the spirit. Beach meals all depend on wind and weather and of course the Earth's latitudes, but they can be used cannily by us. First, find the beach. . . in about 1747 an Englishwoman named Hannah Glasse published her revolutionary *Art of Cookery*, in which she began one recipe by saying something like, "First catch your hare, then cook him." So first find the beach! Then cook on it.

I was lucky as a beacher, because from the first I lived near several coves and stretches, now wall-to-wall-carpeted with people, but then as innocent of them as we were of traffic and singles-motels and suchlike.

I was doubly fortunate because I lived for several months of the year, and always in the summer, with Aunt Gwen, who had been born in the New Zealand bush and knew many secret truths about survival and its delights. My sister and I, with gradual sibling additions, followed wherever this woman led us, somewhat like young aborigines overlaced with Victorian proprieties, and more often than not ate our evening meals on one of the sand stretches or in one of the now private coves of Laguna Beach. We kept one eye on the sunset and the other on our fire.

There was not much driftwood in the summer where the dunes formed themselves further northward. We always chose a spot out of the wind, if there was any, scavenged for dried kelp stems and the twigs we could find along the stretches of ice plant and delicate native succulents that spilled down the cliffs like jewels in those distant days. Sometimes, if we were near home, we carried down a few pieces of discarded lumber. In those times, the fire was small but intense, and delicately monitored for a twig here, a scrap there.

The food was as simple. Usually we each brought a piece or two of bread, warm from our pockets. There would be a weenie apiece, toasted on a light grill we had carried along, or on our own long forks. If the weenie rolled off into the ashes and sand, we ran down to the surf and washed it off and came prancing back to reheat it.

I don't remember drinking anything at these feasts, but the sweet part is strong in my mind, and of course by now it seems difficult to digest empathetically: *marshmallows.* They were part of the ritual for several important years of my life. We speared them on our forks or on long twigs we had trimmed beforehand, and we developed ways of twirling and browning them that can never be duplicated. . . except by every kid in the world who has roasted a marshmallow over a campfire. (There was/is one trick about making a kind of skin on the compact blob of sugar and starches, a brown layer that is offered to any older people around the fire, who must pull it off and eat it, while another one is being twirled into shape over the hot embers. This rite still goes on, and it is chancy and solemn.)

One summer in Laguna we had a car, and I remember carrying a heavy frying pan down into what is now Emerald Bay, and then carrying it up from the beach again, but I don't recall what we cooked in it. It may well have been a steak. There was a lot of dry driftwood in the empty cove, and we had a good fire, and probably we fried pieces of meat. This was a rare occasion, but the skillet was only a bore.

Were there any plates-knives-spoons in those days? We ate what there was with our fingers, and then wiped them clean in the sand, then we doused the embers and stamped them back into the earth much as the New Zealanders must have done. We rubbed off the little grill with more sand, to make it sweet for the next time.

A special part of eating on the beaches near Laguna then was that we learned how to roast kelp. I would like to taste some now. This minute. I know that Japanese friends understand its strange brittle pungency, and it was on the stark beaches of their northern islands that Aunt Gwen learned about it, because her parents were roving medical missionaries and it was a natural progression from New Zealand to Borneo to Japan. . . .

This is not a recipe for the delicacy, but a hint of how it might be done: the long kelp leaves must be washing up on shore very near the surf. Break off leaves about eight to ten inches long, complete with bulbs, from the tail of the plant. Pierce a bulb with the long marshmallow stick or fork, and toast carefully over the embers of a good fire, until the leaf is thoroughly dried and crisp. Break off little hot chips and eat them. They will be delicately coated with salt, which if the sun has not set can be seen glinting whitely. They will be delicious.

In today's patterns of eating, they would be desirable as a kind of pre-meal tidbit with drinks, but they do need a good slow elderly fire, not the blaze that promises further elegancies in beach dining.

I have been to a few so-called beach picnics since my early beacher days, and in spite of my innate astonishment at their complications, I still think it is fun to have people cope with such basics as sand and wind and sudden cold and tidal changes. After a childhood of hunkering over cool sand or digging a hole for my hipbone as I lay on its fading warmth, however, I find it stilted and awkward to stand around with a glass in one hand and plate of something in the other, and even more stilted to see tables and chairs readied on carpets or mats.

But the food still tastes good. How can it not? There is something about salty, moving, shifting tricky air blowing in over the tide-drawn surf that rouses an appetite we never know in closed rooms. We *pounce*, no matter how discreetly! We eat things that may be catered by Malibu's fanciest foodster, but that taste eternally "in" with the extra merciful dash of sea air salt.

Once I went to a beach supper, several decades removed from the kelp-weenie days, where special little wagons were rolled out along the private fifty feet or so of "frontage," on big pneumatic tires that did not sink into the sand nor stir it up. Everything had been calculated with a meteorologist and there was almost no breeze, and we were served not only red caviar (for the properly timed sunset), but crude native-to-Newport dishes like *seviche*. Not a grain of foreign material blew in the Dom Pérignon.

On up the coast from such latter-day glitter, I once crouched in a deep dune-pit near Morro Bay with some other good people, when the wind whistled over us so loudly that everything we ate or drank, even from cans and bottles, was gritty with sand. But we felt warm and happy, and that without a fire in the pale noonday sunlight!

Another noon, near Jenner, a little south of the estuary, we found a noble old drift log and made it a bulwark against the somewhat bitter wind. The sun there was hot, so people stripped off the clothes that had been insurance on the walk down the beach, all of us carrying bags, bundles, baskets.

As I remember, we ate plenty of excellent bread, and bowls of a fish stew based on fresh mussels, and then hearty slabs of an apple tart. There were red and white wines, and then thermos bottles of coffee and tea for the needful. It was a fine, slow, sunny meal, simple in the vocabularies of the people there. We lay like seals in the sun, flapping our fins now and then. Gradually the sunset breeze came onto us, even behind the big old log, and we picked up all the kettles and baskets and headed along the beach toward our cars.

Of course, besides the primeval wish for heat (a little fire or even the charcoal-electric-portable-wide-tired grill), and for food to hold over it and then devour, there is the true beacher's need to smell.

A marshmallow properly toasting over low embers sends out an ineffable whiff of darkening sugar. A leaf of kelp, patiently dried over coals, smells even better, and even more-so at the end of a Gargantuan feast. And many modern beachers know that grilling steaks or ribs will attract a dim haunting ring of faces on the dark beach, other people lured to that lighted spot like wasps to delectable carrion.

One of the best of these smells that I have succumbed to, lately, was in the Old Port in Marseilles, France. It was a fine weekend. A few fishermen were mending nets or painting their rails. People were strolling, before, during and after Mass. It was a day for what is called locally Sunday sailors, and a dozen or so had brought in a nice catch of sardines and had set up a kind of hibachi and were grilling them there, dockside behind a small club fence. The fish came off the little grill and the white wine bottles opened in fast, skilled rhythm, gobbled and guzzled.

Outside the club fence, a lot of us gathered because we could not help it. We did not envy the Sunday sailors because they were on their side and we on ours, they maintaining a small pleasure craft by doing all their own work on it, and we surviving at our own crafts otherwise. All we wanted to do was be where that

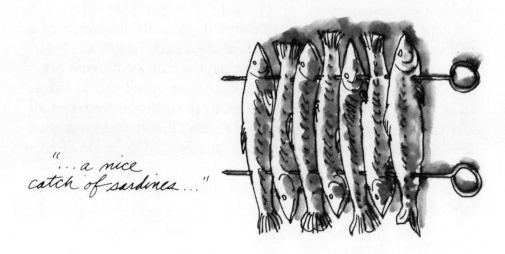

"...a nice catch of sardines..."

smell came from, and lean over the white picket fence and look at people standing up on the cobbles eating grilled just-dead little fishes and drinking just-opened bottles of wine. And so we did, not peevishly but with real enjoyment.

The people off the small yacht knew we were there, and now and then looked up and lifted a glass. We saluted. And the wonderful smell of the sardines grilling over hot coals on the dock nourished us.

Here at home, I sometimes wonder where to go, to recapture this magic. I know a few little kids who toast marshmallows and offer the skins to their elders. I know plenty of beaches. I don't know anybody right now who roasts tender kelp leaves. . . .

I have been told that people in their late teens do not like organized beach meals. Instead, they head for the nearest hamburger huts and chili shacks, and then return to their favorite sands, preferably packed with other lithe brown bodies. And on looking back, I myself remember nothing about building a fire and squatting beside it when I was, say, getting into sixteen. There were so many other things to learn then, about surfing and the differences between boys and girls and all that. Finding wood for a sunset fire was a Cub Scout game, and sitting by its embers with a glass of cold white wine was for the old ones.

Fortunately this phase does not last long in the true beachers, the ones who knew how to nurse a little bed of salty embers before they could read, and keep a weenie from falling off its long fork. If a person really has seven ages to live, the beachers will spend between four and six of them eating sand, no matter how inadvertently, with blissful pleasure at feeling fresh and free and hungry and thirsty.

There can be a big kettle of clams or mussels steaming, or a grill with freshly caught rock fish or even little beefsteaks on it, or a pot of stew. The sunset will perhaps stir up a dark gust of air that lifts sand into a mug, a glass; but the smell of the fire is drink enough, and sand soon settles to the bottom. And a small surfwave will always rinse off a weenie! (This unwritten truism does not hold for a marshmallow, but few *aficionados* of this delicate skin-game worry. . . .)

And now and then there will be fresh kelp on a good, clean stretch of beach, waiting. . . .

CAMP COOKING

■▪■▪■▪■▪■▪■▪■▪■▪■▪■▪■▪■▪■▪■▪■▪■▪■▪■

Recreational camping has had a long history in this country. From the middle of the nineteenth century to the early 1900s it wasn't unusual for people to go camping for a month or more at a time; when these people camped, they *camped*.

A wonderful book by the title of *Camp Kits and Camp Life*, written in 1906 by Charles Stedman Hanks (also the author of *Hints to Golfers*), offers the following advice: "Even in the woods one wants a variety of food, and no one but a tenderfoot any longer thinks being comfortable is being effeminate or that roughing it means putting up with hardships. Don't therefore, be a martyr and suffer discomforts if they can be avoided because some one may think you have no sand. As you will get by shooting and fishing the larger part of what you eat, enough groceries for two men and two guides for a month will be. . ." and he proceeds to list some forty-seven items, with an estimated weight of 362 pounds, and then advises "at the place where you leave the train get two bushels of potatoes, fifteen pounds of salt pork, half a bushel of onions, a fifteen-dozen case of eggs, and three lanterns for candles." Can you imagine the look of the faces of the guides when they saw Mr. Hanks and his group coming?

Times have changed. Not only have camping trips become shorter, but they've become lighter. While many people use a camp stove these days, there's a sizable number who still do, or want to, cook over an open campfire. Mr. Hanks has some good words about the art of building a cookfire:

> Always have a separate fire for the cooking, but don't be an amateur and because wood is plenty have a fire which will roast an ox. Leave some wood for the return trip. Before you begin cooking let the wood burn until there are plenty of live coals. Then poke the pieces which are still giving out a flame to one side for the boiling and stewing, and the hot ashes and live coals for broiling, baking, roasting, and frying. Remember that old camp cooks take all unburnt wood out the fire before they begin to cook, and that the novice is sure to put more on. Remember,

too, that the secret of baking, roasting and frying is a bed of hot coals, and the secret of broiling is a hot bed of hardwood coals.

COOKING OVER WOOD

There is a significant difference between cooking over a wood fire and cooking over a charcoal fire, whether at home or in camp. For the most part, a wood fire will burn hot and fast in the beginning, eventually burning down to a rather short-lived bed of coals (depending, in large part, on the size of the logs the fire was built with—the larger the pieces of wood, the longer it's going to take to get to the red-hot coal stage, but the longer the coals will last).

Cooking over wood demands some skills based on experience. There are two ways around the problem of high heat at first and the short period when the coals are "just right." The first is to

an elaborate set-up for camp cooking.

A simpler method: two green logs, placed at a slight angle to each other, with the fire in between.

start the fire with dry wood, then add some larger green wood which will burn more slowly and evenly (and with less flames), but with more smoke—a by-product you may or may not want. The other is to start the fire with dry wood and then add small pieces of dry hardwood, such as oak, maple, or manzanita. Hardwood tends to produce a better, longer-lived bed of coals than does softwood. It's like the difference between burning a bunch of cardboard, which would flare up in flames only too quickly to disintegrate into ashes, and wood, which catches fire fairly quickly but takes longer to burn itself completely out. The general rule is, the denser the composition of the material being burned, the longer it will burn or stay hot; hence hardwoods produce a better bed of coals than do softwoods.

ZEN AND THE ART OF FIRE-BUILDING

As a unique talent, it is not surprising that our illustrator, Earl Thollander, has a unique method of building a wood fire that can be adapted to use at the beach or in the campground. Earl moved to his property, located above Calistoga at the northernmost end of the Napa Valley in California, in 1964. His house sits on a hill in the middle of a forest. Before moving to the house on Murray Hill from San Francisco, Earl had never taken an interest in outdoor grilling. As it happens, the previous owners left him with the rather picturesque stone grill and fireplace you see illustrated on the cover of this book. Earl now estimates that he grills every other day except in the dead of winter. Although he claims not to be an expert, twenty years of consistent practice has its rewards.

Earl starts his fire with newspaper and is a self-proclaimed "crumpler." On top of the crumpled newspaper ("not too tight—leave plenty of room for air"), he adds a layer of dry twigs. After lighting the paper on fire he quickly adds a layer of bigger, dry wood (½ to 1 inch in diameter). After the fire has had a chance to become quite hot, he adds a few pieces of slightly larger (¾ to 1½ inches in diameter) recently cut wood—that is, wood that is still slightly green. Once the flames are directed nicely up towards the chimney he puts the meal on the grill, to sear in the juices of whatever it is he happens to be grilling while the fire is still very hot, and turns the meat once. The basic difference between using wood, rather than charcoal, is that a wood fire tends to die down much more quickly. Earl has adapted his grilling method to his fuel; as the fire rapidly dies down to glowing embers, he moves the grill closer to the coals to finish the cooking process.

Earl says that he takes particular satisfaction in cooking a meal over fuel that comes from his own property; he has never used charcoal briquets, charcoal starter, or any other commercially available product. Earl notes, "As the most primitive way to start a fire, and subsequently cook a meal, this is also the most appealing. I think there must be some Zen in there."

EPILOGUE

Type A and B behavior have been well chronicled of late. With the publication of this book, I thought it might be time to identify yet another behavior pattern, namely Type C — C for charcoal, of course.

Type C behavior is, according to the most recent surveys, characterized by equal parts hedonism and a sort of wholesale Zen approach to life. "Could this person be serious?" you may be saying to yourself about now. In all earnestness, yes. As I write these words, on a warm evening in the midst of a splendid Indian summer, the sun is reaching through a towering elm. Its rays, which take on a curious orange glow about this time, find their way to an old Japanese maple, working the texture into a magical tapestry of light, color, and shadow. The colors of the sun lick around the chunks of mesquite burning in preparation for the evening meal. The almost electric whine of two humming-birds and the chirp of the towhees, which seem to sing only just prior to sunrise and sunset, elicit attention and partially obscure the sounds of buses and motorcycles in the distance.

As for hedonism, there's an enormous slab of ribs, dusted with plenty of cracked pepper and paprika, on a large Blue Willow platter garnished with a couple of sprigs of parsley, a bowl of time-tested and -honored hot sauce, a basting brush, and, yes, a frosty, very dry Gibson (two onions, please).

To Type C people everywhere, I raise my glass. Here's to the primal pleasures of home and hearth, pleasures that help to see us through from one day to the next. And now as the sun sets and the crickets take up their late-summer chorus, it's time to have another short one and get those ribs on the grill.

—A. Cort Sinnes

INDEX

COOKBOOKS FROM ARIS BOOKS

The Book of Garlic by Lloyd J. Harris. A compilation of recipes, lore, history, medicinal concoctions, and much more. "Admirably researched and well written."—Craig Claiborne in *The New York Times*. 286 pages, paper $9.95.

The International Squid Cookbook by Isaac Cronin. A charming collection of recipes and culinary information. 96 pages, paper $7.95.

Mythology and Meatballs: A Greek Island Diary/Cookbook by Daniel Spoerri. A marvelous, magical travel/gastronomic diary with fascinating recipes, anecdotes, and mythologies. 238 pages, cloth $16.95, paper $10.95.

The California Seafood Cookbook by Isaac Cronin, Jay Harlow, and Paul Johnson. The definitive recipe and reference guide to fish and shellfish of the Pacific. 288 pages, cloth $20.00, paper $12.95.

The Feast of the Olive by Maggie Blyth Klein. A complete recipe and reference guide to using fine olive oils and a variety of cured olives. 223 pages, cloth $16.95, paper $10.95.

The Art of Filo Cookbook by Marti Sousanis. International entrées, appetizers, and desserts wrapped in flaky pastry. 144 pages, paper $9.95.

Chèvre! The Goat Cheese Cookbook by Laurel Chenel and Linda Siegfried. A marvelous collection of international recipes using goat cheese. 119 pages, paper $9.95.

Ginger East to West by Bruce Cost. A complete, fascinating reference guide to ginger—its mystique, history, and important role in international cuisine. Includes over 80 marvelous recipe. 192 pages, cloth $17.95, paper $10.95.

From a Baker's Kitchen by Gail Sher. A comprehensive guide to the art of baking. 224 pages, paper $11.95.

Chef Wolfe's New American Turkey Cookery by Ken Wolfe and Olga Bier. Carefully illustrated techniques, delicious recipes, and basic culinary sense bring our all-American bird into the 21st century. 156 pages, paper $8.95.

Compliments of the Chef by The Sisterhood of Beth El with Paul Johnston. 100 great recipes from the innovative restaurants and cafes of Berkeley, California. 160 pages, paper $9.95.

To receive the above titles, send a check or money order for the amount of the book plus $1.50 postage and handling for the first title, and 75¢ for each additional title, to Aris Books, 1621 Fifth St., Berkeley, CA 94710. California residents add 6.5% sales tax.